THE
GOD
OF
STORY

THE GOD
OF
STORY

DISCOVERING THE NARRATIVE
OF SCRIPTURE THROUGH
THE LANGUAGE OF STORYTELLING

DANIEL SCHWABAUER

BakerBooks

a division of Baker Publishing Group
Grand Rapids, Michigan

Published by Baker Books
a division of Baker Publishing Group
Grand Rapids, Michigan
BakerBooks.com

Printed in the United States of America

Library of Congress Cataloging-in-Publication Data
Names: Schwabauer, Daniel, author.
Title: The God of story : discovering the narrative of scripture through the language of storytelling / Daniel Schwabauer.
Description: Grand Rapids, Michigan : Baker Books, a division of Baker Publishing Group, [2025] | Includes bibliographical references.
Identifiers: LCCN 2024016036 | ISBN 9781540904638 (paper) | ISBN 9781540904768 (casebound) | ISBN 9781493449132 (ebook)
Subjects: LCSH: Storytelling—Religious aspects—Christianity. | Bible—Criticism, Narrative. | Narration in the Bible.
Classification: LCC BT83.78 .S45 2025 | DDC 220.6—dc23/eng/20240605
LC record available at https://lccn.loc.gov/2024016036

Cover design by John Lucas

Baker Publishing Group publications use paper produced from sustainable forestry practices and postconsumer waste whenever possible.

25 26 27 28 29 30 31   7 6 5 4 3 2 1

CONTENTS

PLOT

CONCLUSION

FOREWORD

More Than an Inkling

The table was not open to everyone, only those with certain inklings. First, you had to be a Christian, an intellectual, and an active writer who lived in the Oxford area in the 1930s and 1940s. Second, you had to believe in the power of story to change the world and the pivotal role of "myth" as something that never was but always is. Third, you had to be enamored of the grandness of children's imaginations as glimmers of dawn. Those were the entrance requirements to meet each week in a home or pub to talk about storylines, myth, and hope.

The group informally went by the adopted title "The Inklings." It included academic luminaries such as J. R. R. Tolkien, Charles Williams, C. S. Lewis, J. A. W. Bennett, Lord David Cecil, and Owen Barfield. These intellectuals wanted to move beyond mere philosophical fiddle, however arrant and adroit, and theological faddle, however inerrant and pitch-perfect, and enter the Elysium fields of yarn, yore, and yonder.

As you will discover in this radiant book, Daniel Schwabauer is an Inkling in every way but historical. He shows us how stories are reality-bending creatures. How do you grow a faith that is abiding, deepening, ripening in love and maturing in truth, nourished by Scripture and sacrament? Truth-telling is story-telling. If you could just "say" the truth, it wouldn't be truth. Truth is something (or for the Christian, truth is Someone) you "do" more than "say." You enact and embody moments of truth.

The solution to life's biggest problems, the answer to life's hardest questions, is story. But not just any story—the story of Jesus. To pass on the "headline news" of good news is to pass on a story—the story of Jesus racked on a cross, risen, rising, regnant, and returning. This era of cultural climate change is in such desperate need of alternative narratives, as Schwabauer demonstrates. How about giving it the Jesus story? It's a life-giving story that changes everything.

On June 10, 1963, President John F. Kennedy gave a speech at American University in Washington, DC. Kennedy instructed his speechwriter Ted Sorensen to draft him a speech that would call for an end to the nuclear arms race and a test ban treaty and that would summon a new era. Seven months after the Cuban Missile Crisis, and less than six months before he would be assassinated, President Kennedy hoped this speech would change the course of history. Emboldened by Pope John XXIII, who while dying of cancer was spending his last breaths behind the scenes bringing Kennedy and Khrushchev together and writing his papal encyclical *Pacem in Terris*, Kennedy told his American University audience that all humans share the same story. "In the final analysis, our most basic common link is that we all inhabit this small planet. We all breathe the same air. We all cherish our children's future. And we are all mortal."[1]

As I was being hypnotized while reading *The God of Story*, I was haunted by the sense that I had been similarly mesmerized before by someone's writing. But where? And who? Then it hit me, and a conviction grew in me that Daniel Schwabauer has the makings of being the next Frederick Buechner. This is high praise since I view Buechner as one of the greatest communicators since Jesus. Both Schwabauer and Buechner have that same inimitable ability to pick up a metaphor, as Jesus did, take it for a walk, and weave from the "sacred journey" a narrative that heals into holiness and hastens the kingdom.

In the early 1990s, the Trinity Institute invited Buechner to join Maya Angelou in giving a lecture series on the subject of story. Buechner balked. In his words, story was "the big fad in theology, and when I hear it, it just drives me mad."[2] In Buechner's view, story was being co-opted by the advertising and marketing worlds to sell things that had become substitutes for substance. But after a personal intercession he eventually consented to come, and he agreed to speak first.

After Buechner had shared his spiritual autobiography, he turned the podium over to Maya Angelou. The master of ceremonies introducing Angelou said, "Ms. Angelou will now get up and tell you her story, and it will be a very different story from the one that you have just heard from Frederick Buechner." As she walked to the dais, Angelou shook her head from side to side. The first words out of her mouth corrected the host who introduced her: "I have exactly the same story to tell as Frederick Buechner." To quote Buechner, at the level of humanity, and in spite of all our differences, "We all have the same story, and therefore anybody's story can illuminate our own."[3]

In the pages of this book you will find many inklings that these words are more true than you thought: we all share the same story, and our stories have the power to transport us to different worlds, to teach us new things about our world, and to birth a new world. Or in Daniel Schwabauer's resounding words, "The language of that [the Jesus] story is not just the language of humanity; it is the language of life."

Leonard Sweet
Author, professor, and publisher

9

INTRODUCTION

My Summer on Mars

No one believes me when I tell them I've been to Mars.

It happened during the summer of 1977, just after I graduated from the fifth grade.

My father had taken a job as the project manager for a massive building project in downtown Tulsa. Dad didn't want to spend the whole summer separated from his family, so he bought an 18-foot Coleman camper and told us to pack what we needed for a summer in Oklahoma.

To me this meant a baseball glove and a stack of books. Just before leaving town I fortuitously discovered *A Princess of Mars* in a friend's basement library and was sent off on my journey with a grocery bag full of old pulp novels.

We landed at a KOA outside the city limits, beyond even the suburbs, a quarter mile from the highway. The place felt like Mars to me: brutally hot days and cool, breezy nights; a barren landscape of sharp-edged rocks and fine dust that swirled underfoot and clung to everything; a sea of red stretching to the horizon. From the porthole window of my narrow top bunk above the tool chest and spare tire, I could see the rim of a dry canal bending into the distance.

Fortunately, our environmental shelter came equipped with air-conditioning and a built-in reading light, making the transition from Earth to Barsoom ridiculously easy. For eleven weeks I whiled away the hours absorbed in books written by a man who had taken so many readers to Mars that eventually a crater was named after him.

Edgar Rice Burroughs is best known as the creator of *Tarzan of the Apes*, but his John Carter of Mars series was far more intriguing to me than his jungle hero.

Since that miraculous summer I have reread *A Princess of Mars* several times, always hoping to recapture a little of the magic. I am always disappointed. The book simply wasn't written for a twenty-first-century adult.

But it's not just Edgar Rice Burroughs who disappoints. Few of the stories that engaged me as a child hold my interest now. I am too cynical, too fat with stories, too old for the common wonder of childhood.

I wish I could reenter the fantastical places I slipped into so easily when I was younger. I wish I could go to Mars again. But growing up has consequences.

As the brain develops, we find different things appealing. The desire for wonder is supplanted by a drive for romance and sex, for human drama, and for insight into the nature of things. Life experience begins to hammer home the painful differences between fantasy and reality. In short, the kinds of stories we crave become more logical, more informative, more true to life.

This, as I said, is disappointing. I want to believe in the green men of Mars and their tusky cavalries. I want to ride a sky ship and bound across the Martian soil with a six-legged dog. I want to be insanely good with a saber in spite of the fact I've never actually taken lessons or even held one.

But I am old enough now to have learned that life isn't like that.

Which could lead me to the tempting conclusion that life is an existential letdown. The future was supposed to be better than this. More awe-inspiring. More evolved. I was promised a jetpack and regular vacations to the moon. Instead, life handed me a second mortgage and a spontaneous allergy to gluten.

Is it, then, all a trick? Are fairy tales just the soft lies we tell children to protect them from truths they are not yet prepared to face? Was the innocence of childhood nothing more than a happy dream?

This book is my attempt to answer that question fairly and with great hope.

I hope to demonstrate that all stories—even the dreamy fantasies of childhood—point to something bigger than entertainment or even survival, and that, properly understood, the language of story is the language of Scripture.

To demonstrate the latter, I lean heavily on three techniques that may not be familiar to readers. Indeed, the first of these is *defamiliarization*, particularly the defamiliarization of the Bible. As long as we come to its text thinking we already know what's there, we're unlikely to see anything new or inspiring or revelatory. And there is always something life-changing in it, provided we're willing to be challenged. The difficulty lies in the fact that our Bible cups are already filled. We know the stories of the forbidden fruit, of the Red Sea parting, of baby Jesus asleep in a manger. To really appreciate these and other narratives in Scripture, we must learn to turn them over, see them from a fresh angle, and shake them free of their familiar wrappings. To be filled, our cups must first be emptied.

Art, after all, is a way of revealing the hidden things we dismiss or take for granted in reality. Great art hides its most profound revelations in ways that provoke curiosity and compel us to look closer. In other words, it uses an *abductive* process, the second technique explored in this book. Abductive storytelling is outlined more thoroughly in chapter 2.

Finally, I rely on a simple and repeated invitation to place *yourself* in the stories of the Bible. Not as its protagonist, but as someone whose life has been interrupted by a startling breaking-in of God's kingdom: a good man whose quiet life is targeted by demonic forces; a prophet whose life and identity are turned upside-down; a blind man whose sight is restored.

Stories are important because they demonstrate that ultimate meaning exists. Not only does it exist, but it is sometimes wondrous, often horrifying, and occasionally funny.

This book was written for everyone who has been to Mars or Narnia or Middle-earth and discovered you were more at home there than you are here.

This book was written for everyone who longs for home.

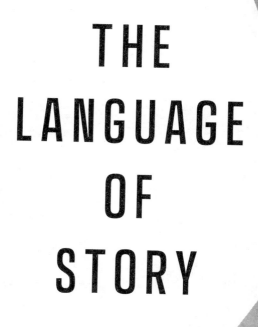

THE
LANGUAGE
OF
STORY

1

THE GREAT PYRAMID

The Western church has a story problem. Because story lies at the heart of Christianity, this problem represents an existential crisis. Yet few are even aware that a crisis exists.

Put simply, we do not understand how stories work. We neither study nor teach the language of story, nor do we recognize the foundational truths embedded in its grammar. We don't appreciate the role story plays in human development, and we barely acknowledge its importance to the shaping of culture. Somehow the church has forgotten what we once almost took for granted—that life is a story.

If life is a story, it can only be rightly understood in story terms. But how are we to understand those terms when we consistently disregard and devalue them?

American evangelicals in particular have largely abandoned the arts. Our sermons, community dramas, religious novels, and Christian films often reject subtlety in narration and instead mount an assault on the rational mind that is direct, clear, and lifeless. Consequently, our attempts to use the language of story as a delivery mechanism for the gospel have about as much emotional impact as a doctor's needle. Rather than pursuing Thomas Aquinas's coherence of beauty, goodness, and truth, our storytellers project sterile, propositional truths stripped of goodness and beauty. Such stories are virtually useless when it comes to conveying the gospel of Christ to the culture.

Furthermore, our naive approach to story as a needle-and-serum delivery mechanism of two components, story and message, leaves us vulnerable to the subtle manipulation of certain non-Christian storytellers who are quite adept at utilizing narratives to persuade, manipulate, and control. Ever on the lookout for toxic injections of bad messaging, we inflate the danger of movies and books with a transparent political agenda while overlooking the more insidious content that can subtly reshape an audience's worldview through a deft use of ideals (moral standards).[1] Somehow we've forgotten that the serpent was more crafty than the other creatures (Gen. 3:1).

Maybe the worst thing about our failure to learn and to teach the language of story is that we don't understand our own Scriptures. The Bible isn't written in just Hebrew, Aramaic, and Greek. It's also written in story. Its layered narratives, metaphors, and poetic images are endlessly rich, its structures and arcs and dramatic connections profoundly meaningful. They are indeed treasures worth seeking (Matt. 13:52). But unless we learn to see the Scriptures through this lens—unless we humble ourselves as little children begging for a story—we will never fully understand the depths or the elegance of God's Word. Theologian Leonard Sweet writes:

> Story is the flesh and blood of life. And the body of Christ needs to be fed with the stories of the gospel—stories that shock and stories that twist around our self-concerned notions and

18

expectations and leave us naked, confused, witless, and willing to let God lead us into new pastures.[2]

This book is therefore an attempt to explore what we seem to have forgotten. Each section is divided into two chapters. The first chapter in each pairing explores one essential narrative principle; the second applies that principle to the Bible. Chapter 12 is my attempt to provide a summarizing narrative framework for the story of Scripture through the life of Jesus.

His story is not just the resolution of the biblical narrative. It is the *singularity*—the infinite value—to which all stories point.

A Baptism in Story

This structural pairing of chapters into practical twins of theory and application is deeply personal to me because it mirrors so much of my journey as a young Christian navigating the academic world.

Though I was raised in a devout Lutheran home, it was not until I lived off-campus during my undergraduate studies at the University of Kansas that I encountered Christ personally. My grandfather had just passed away from cancer, and it terrified me to see his once-imposing frame shriveled down to a ninety-pound husk. Then my father had a series of strokes and heart attacks that left him fighting for his life at a local hospital. The doctors told us he wouldn't make it. As he still lay speechless and barely conscious, I received similarly grim news—a diagnosis of spinal cancer that needed further confirmation. Back then the waiting period for an MRI was several months long, so I spent the interim reading religious texts in the hope of finding some sort of consolation.

I read the Bhagavad Gita and the Upanishads. I read Lao Tzu and Confucius. I read many New Age writers, including Richard Bach and others who claimed to have secret knowledge of the afterlife. At one point I even read newsletters from the Rosicrucians. This happened well before such information was easily accessible online; the university library still used an enormous cabinet for its card catalog, and circulation still involved stamping physical cards.

None of the reading helped, though it did broaden my horizons enough to reinforce how little I knew about anything. I had spent years training to be a martial artist and was physically fit and mentally agile. Just weeks before, my whole life had stretched ahead as an implied promise of marriage and children and career. I knew how things were supposed to unfold, and though I understood that sometimes tragedy strikes, I was overwhelmed by the reality that my hopes and dreams and even my life could be stripped away so quickly.

One evening, at a point of extreme hopelessness when I was alone in an off-campus apartment, I reached for the Bible my other grandfather, a Lutheran minister, had left me. Flipping to the words in red, I began to read them as if for the first time. What struck me with particular impact was the contrast between everything Jesus said and everything I'd been reading. Lao Tzu, Confucius, Bach, and all the rest spoke like good men with good ideas. But Jesus spoke like he *knew* something. His words had a weight that continually made me stop reading, as if I could only carry them for a few minutes before stopping to rest.

Two things I read that night struck me with the force of a sledgehammer. The first was Matthew 5:27–28: "You have heard that it was said, 'You shall not commit adultery.' But I tell you that anyone who looks at a woman lustfully has already committed adultery with her in his heart."

I was a young man at a state school and surrounded by over twelve thousand young women who were themselves exploring adulthood. I wasn't supposed to notice the short skirts and tank tops? How could any normal, hormonal nineteen-year-old guy regulate his imagination so strictly that he never entertained sexual thoughts? And what sort of God was this who applied such a harsh, seemingly impossible standard? Hadn't he made me the way I was?

But when I continued reading, I came across Matthew 11:11 and had to stop again: "Truly I tell you, among those born of women there has not risen anyone greater than John the Baptist; yet whoever is least in the kingdom of heaven is greater than he."

I knew about John the Baptist. The church I'd attended growing up boasted a stained glass window depicting his beheading. If Christ's first standard about lust had been outrageous, this one even was more so, but in the opposite direction. Somehow I understood not the theology of this promise but the beauty of what lay behind it: following Jesus would elevate me above even the most holy of ancient prophets. I was being asked to surrender everything that made me what I considered myself, and in exchange I would gain—what? Well, Jesus, I supposed. That was the deal. Lay down my old life; pick up a new one. Let go of my right to things like lust and pride and preferring my own way. And in return?

I wish I could say that I saw all this clearly, but my discomfort was more the conviction of a problem than the assurance of a solution. I didn't decide to follow Jesus because I believed in him. I decided to follow him because I saw that it was either him or nothing.

With no understanding of a "prayer of salvation," I knelt on the cheap carpet and said, as best I can recall it, "Jesus, I don't know if you're there or not. I just know that if you're not God, there is no God. It's you or nothing. So I'm going to spend my life following you, even if you're not there. The thing is, I'm a hypocrite, and I know I will never make it on my own. If you *are* there, I need you to help me. I want to be the least in your kingdom. Make me your water boy."

That last request made sense to me at the time because I felt such overwhelming unworthiness. Who was I to take the same field as John the Baptist or the disciples? But a water boy? A water boy was only in the dugout because he knew somebody. He didn't have to be talented or athletic.

I suppose I expected God to hear me, but in my imagination, prayer was like leaving a message on God's answering machine. It was something he took note of, perhaps much later, and either tossed in the trash or nodded at begrudgingly.

To my astonishment, the Spirit of God descended into that room so forcefully that it took my breath away. I saw no visions and heard no angelic choirs, but I could feel the peace of God draping over me like a weighted blanket, and the heaviness of it pressed me into the floor. *He's real!* I thought. *He's really real! And he's here! I can't believe it!*

Like Nathanael, I didn't believe in Jesus until I met him. And then everything changed.

I started going to a young men's discipleship group and then to church. I began reading the Bible and trying to pray. And I started asking awkward questions in my English classes.

For the next few years, I lived not a double life but a parallel life. I lived as a pariah in the academic world—the born-again Christian who found postmodern literature to be meaningless and depressing. And in church circles I was the college writing nerd who didn't understand why the stories in the Bible had to be read in the most lifeless way imaginable. So I learned to move quietly between the contrasting cultures of academia and ecclesia, of hopeless entertainment and befuddled expectation.

It took me decades of study and prayer to begin to understand what lay at the heart of this division.

The world has forgotten that stories work because they point to God, to the Sender of ultimate meaning. The basic elements of every story are whispering to us, in narrative form, about a reality that is larger than a purely material cosmos.

Evangelicals have forgotten that before it's anything else, God's story is a narrative, and that to be understood the Bible must be experienced as such.

What both groups need is to be baptized in the language of story.

The Great Pyramid

Most readers will already be familiar with the five basic story elements: characterization, plot, context, theme, and voice. But each of these concepts is more significant than even your high school English teacher may have led you to believe. Not only do they inform and shape our maturation into adulthood, they also connect us with the generations that came before us and those that will follow after. Story grounds us in history.

The perennial elements of story form an emotional grammar that points both to human experience and to a divine origin. Because the elements exist wherever stories are told, they are useful—indeed, they are essential—in crossing the gulf of time that separates modern readers from biblical stories. The ancient Hebrew- and Greek-writing authors who crafted the Scriptures may have lived with different cultural values, recognized different character archetypes, and assumed different contextual themes than we do, but it is inarguable (and wondrous) that they told stories built around settings, characters, and themes. The story of King Solomon, for instance, shares profound structural similarities with Shakespeare's *Macbeth*.

In *The Storytelling Animal*, Jonathan Gottschall describes the ubiquity of story throughout history:

No matter how far we travel back into the literary history, and no matter how deep we plunge into the jungles and badlands

23

of world folklore, we always find the same astonishing thing: *their stories are just like ours.* There is a universal grammar in world fiction, a deep pattern of heroes confronting trouble and struggling to overcome.

But there is more to this grammar than the similarities in skeletal structure; there are also similarities in the flesh. As many scholars of world literature have noted, stories revolve around a handful of master themes.[3]

The fact that biblical narratives work as stories—and are understandable as such—provides us with what may be our greatest interpretive gift. Yet it is a gift that remains largely unopened.

Perhaps this reluctance to explore the biblical narratives as stories shouldn't be surprising. Humans, after all, have a talent for dismissing anything that doesn't align with our existing assumptions, no matter how obvious or colossal its presence.

The Great Pyramid of Giza, for instance, stands clearly visible for miles. Yet it was largely misunderstood for over fifteen hundred years. Napoleon Bonaparte led an expedition to Egypt in 1798 that marked the first major attempt to understand the structure as designed. The entrance lay hidden by sand, with only the corner steps carved from bedrock indicating the pyramid's base. When Napoleon ordered 250 soldiers and hired workers to start digging, the entrance was eventually exposed, thus permitting the clearing of the pyramid's descending passage and chambers. We're told, "After making his way up into the King's Chamber, Napoleon asked to be left alone for a while. He is reputed to have been unwilling or unable ever to answer those who asked him what he had experienced."[4]

No amount of digging, however, could untangle the mysteries of the strange writings around the tombs in the Valley of the Kings. The ability to read hieroglyphics had died out in the fourth century AD and wouldn't be relearned until well after the discovery of the Rosetta Stone, which occurred in 1799 during this same Napoleonic expedition.

The Rosetta Stone provided the key to hieroglyphics because it presented nearly identical information in three separate languages: ancient Greek, Demotic, and hieroglyphic script. Still, it took several decades before scholars were able to confidently translate it. Meanwhile, some explorers rejected what they found written on stone in Egypt because when looking at hieroglyphics they didn't see text.

For roughly fifteen hundred years nobody in the world understood the looming structures at Giza, even though their purpose was deeply meaningful on multiple levels. An ancient treasure—too large to miss—glowed in the desert sun, its slope perfectly mirroring the angle of sunlight breaking through clouds, but not a single human knew that the Great Pyramid was itself a giant hieroglyph. And why? Because its foundation was hidden and its foundational language was forgotten.

We evangelicals are a lot like the generations of travelers who visited Egypt before Napoleon. We puzzle faithfully over the hieroglyphic patterns of Scripture, sensing that something deeper must have been intended but unable to read the writing on the wall. We hold up the Bible as an artifact of sacred history, the colossus of our faith, but do not venture inside.

In truth, we *can't* crawl into its inner chambers because we lack the necessary tools. We don't recognize the corner steps or the markers of the subterranean entry. Without the language of story, we can't read its true meaning or even recognize that our Great Pyramid *is* a hieroglyph. The Bible isn't just a collection of stories. It is *the* story—the one true story to which all are invited.

This is the nature of our problem: We lack the ability to recognize that we lack an ability. We think we understand story, but we don't.

The Language of Story

Very well. We must start somewhere. To understand the depth of our story problem and how to correct it, we must first answer this question: *What are stories for?*

This is no small task.

Narrative theorists tend to propose answers based on evolutionary processes. Some argue that story is a tool of sexual selection; others that it is a method of transmitting culture; still others that it has no meaning at all but is merely a form of chemical addiction, more vestigial tail than asset. These theories all assume that story is a tool for survival. Jonathan Gottschall, echoing the work of child psychologists, suggests that, because stories are almost always about people with problems, they probably exist as virtual tests for future situations. He writes,

> Just as flight simulators allow pilots to train safely, stories safely train us for the big challenges of the social world. Like a flight simulator, fiction projects us into intense simulations of problems that run parallel to those we face in reality. And like a flight simulator, the main virtue of fiction is that we have a rich experience and don't die at the end.[5]

According to this idea, story prepares us to deal with real-world situations by forcing us to imagine them in advance. This is why story can be reduced to a simple equation like Gottschall's:

Story = Character + Predicament + Attempted Extraction[6]

Or, to put it like a creative writing teacher, every story is about a character who is searching for the solution to a problem.

As a writer I sometimes find this definition useful because *problem* and *solution* are really just different ways of saying *conflict* and *resolution*. But if this definition merely means that all stories must have a character and a plot, it isn't saying very much—and it is leaving out theme, voice, and context.

Gottschall's equation is therefore too reductionistic for our purposes here. Any story boiled down to a problem/solution pattern will not retain its power. That I once ran out of gas and had to walk to the nearest filling station is an anecdote, not a story. Though it's built around a protagonist seeking the solution to a problem, it lacks voice, setting, and a motivating force, which robs it of theme. Had I run out of gas and then braved a minefield in order to take a child to safety, I might have the basis of a story. The difference isn't just complexity but the presence of other essential elements that add dramatic tension and therefore interest. Yes, you can make lemonade with just lemon juice and water, but without sweetener is it really lemonade?

But there are two larger problems with the idea that story is an evolutionary flight simulator.

First, enduring stories rarely provide the precise solution to a precise problem. Though it's true that in a story the problem of a dragon may require the solution of a Saint George, this pattern isn't what such stories are *about*. Instead, the problem/solution pattern exists to introduce the necessary endpoints of plot—*conflict* and *resolution*. You can tell this is true by asking if the solutions found in most stories would work in real life. Is the solution to poverty, for instance, that I sell my last cow and buy magic beans from a stranger? Is the problem of wicked stepsisters best solved by the appearance of a fairy godmother? Are saints really the best people to handle real-world dragons?

Second, if stories are just survival-based flight simulators for reality, why do stories usually have at their heart some moral dilemma that directly opposes a survival-of-the-fittest paradigm? I don't mean that good stories moralize. I mean that all stories depend on the existence of a moral compass shared by storyteller and audience. Without such a compass no story can make sense. It is this compass that dictates the true theme of a story; whereas the compass is always relevant, a problem and its solution are generally *least* effective where they are clearly mirrored in reality.

In fairy tales, what makes a problem effective dramatically is not that it's solved by some practical, everyday wisdom, but rather that it's solved through some moral but impractical decision. *Jack and the Beanstalk* isn't about fixing one's finances. Its hero doesn't demonstrate a useful way to survive starvation. Instead, the story shows us what courage looks like: risking everything on a dream of magic, climbing an impossible ladder into the clouds, and plundering the domain of the powerful when everything is stacked against you. "Fee, fie, foe, fum! I smell the blood of an Englishman!" is memorable because of its rhythmic near-rhyme, but its meaning is simple: Jack smells like an Englishman because he reeks of courage. Courage is in his blood. (Though if it were truly in the blood, would English boys need a story reminding them of the fact?) Jack's courage is reckless and foolhardy and absolutely impractical. Yet we admire it because we recognize in it a virtue that's worth seeking—even at the cost of one's life.

This is why I say that effective stories don't serve as flight simulators for life, showing us how we must behave in order to survive. Rather, they show us how we *ought* to behave even if the consequences turn out to be deadly. If story is a flight simulator, it is a terrible one, for it is telling us to land the plane upside down.

Why We Tell Stories

So, what *is* story for if not survival?

Stories exist to preserve and communicate truths that are counterintuitive or contrary to our natural inclinations. They function as vaults for the safeguarding of meaning and of moral precepts. They communicate ideals like courage and honesty, which are *not* explicit in nature and are therefore easy to overlook, misunderstand, or devalue.

Stories tell us that life is meaningful, and at their best they show us how to go about finding that meaning for ourselves. But their method of doing so is neither deductive nor formulaic. Instead, they teach through indirect emotional resonance, or what C. S. Lewis called "classes of experience."[7]

Every story is a journey of exploration that works through a three-part progression of *entertainment, concealment,* and *revelation.* These three traits are how stories preserve and communicate the sorts of truths most challenged by the struggles of life.

Entertainment: Before a story can transform us, it must engage our emotions. Stories always have as their first goal to entertain and delight. Boring stories fail as stories because they don't stimulate the emotions. By definition boredom is the lack of stimulation. Thus, any story that brings enjoyment to the audience has succeeded on its most basic level. Many commercially successful stories aim no higher than this.

Concealment: Great stories are vaults. They conceal truth in order to make sure it is valued and protected. They conceal truth to keep it out of the hands of the so-called wrong people, such as children or those for whom it is eventually intended, *but not yet.* Like Christmas presents hidden in a parent's closet, some truths are best suited for a future date. A story that conceals its theme in the actions of its characters and plot ensures that it will linger in the audience's mind. The head-scratching nature of a well-designed story invites the truth-seeking audience to ponder it and search for its meaning. Those who finally understand what has been hidden inside will delight in telling it to others. Thus it is preserved.

Revelation: Finally, stories reveal truth by presenting it as drama that proves through action, albeit imaginary, some premise or larger truth. The parallel nature of story allows the storyteller to create what fantasy writer Diana Wynne Jones describes as "a mental map—in bold colors or stark black-and-whites—of right and wrong and life as it *should* be."[8]

Stories, in other words, are like the pyramids at Giza—simultaneously explicit and cryptic.

Fairy tales may be the best examples of strong but subtle storytelling because they typically conceal their theme in ways that ensure they are passed on from generation to generation.

Cinderella, for instance, buries its life experience in layers so charming and elemental that its point can be easy to miss even by those who love it the most. Consider the following plot points from *Cinderella*:

1. Wicked stepsisters and a forthcoming ball.
2. The fairy godmother and the magic coach, dress, etc.
3. "Don't stay past midnight."
4. The magic wears off and she loses a glass slipper.
5. The prince identifies Cinderella when the slipper fits her foot.

Two questions about these highlights suggest a theme. First, how does the story actually resolve? And second, if the magic ends at midnight, why is the slipper still there?

Clearly the story resolves when Cinderella marries the prince and finds suitable husbands for her wicked stepsisters, who are transformed by her generosity. Therefore it is likely that the point of the fairy godmother's magic was to bring together two people from different stations who could not otherwise have married.

This in turn suggests an answer to the second question, which is that all the magic certainly *doesn't* end. The part that brings them together—the single glass slipper—remains. Therefore the theme of *Cinderella* might be something like: *The magic of love doesn't wholly last, but it does reveal what's truly there.*

Cinderella, like other great fairy tales, is probably not limited to a theme so clear and simple as this. But such exercises are useful in helping us catch a glimpse of the King's Chamber at its heart.

Little Red Riding Hood is another helpful illustration. Its plot highlights are typically recalled as follows:

1. Red's encounter with the polite wolf.
2. The wolf runs ahead and swallows Red's grandmother.
3. The wolf in Grandmother's nightclothes.
4. "What big eyes . . . ears . . . teeth you have!"
5. A woodcutter rescues Red and her grandmother.

Three questions will prove instructive: How does the story resolve? Why doesn't the wolf eat Red sooner? At what point are children in the audience most enthralled?

This last question is helpful in explaining why the tale re-lies on a deus ex machina ending (in which the main character is helped out of her situation by an outside force). *Little Red Riding Hood* doesn't draw its power from its plot but from its cleverly concealed theme. That theme is most evident at step 4, where an audience of children is most engrossed in Red's unfold-ing horror. *They* know it's a wolf, but Red doesn't. So children are gripped by a progression of threes that leads inevitably to a revelation of just how bad things can be when you trust the wrong person. This idea is reinforced by, and explains the necessity of, the wolf's earlier politeness: *Predators are only nice when they want something from you.*

The key here is that step 4 dramatizes a certain type of experience we might call the death of innocence. Its tension isn't understood by most children, but adults unconsciously empathize with Red's plight. We've all been there. And because we've all been there, we find in the story something important and true and meaningful. Something worth passing on. When we had our run-in with the wolf, there was nothing we could do about it either. It took a woodcutter breaking into our life to pry us from the jaws of destruction.

Drawing the Wrong Conclusion

It must be said that not every story is honest. Any language can be used to lie, and the language of story is no different. Some of our most powerful stories have at their heart either comforting half-truths or outright deception. Fortunately, dishonest stories have three distinguishing characteristics: (1) they make explicit what ought to be implied; (2) they are internally inconsistent; and (3) they violate the language of story by pairing incompatible ideals.

These traits of dishonest stories will become clearer as we unpack the five core elements of story, but an example from *Grimm's Fairy Tales* will reveal how the language of story can be twisted. In this case, we turn to *Hansel and Gretel* for its dark but highly memorable outline.

1. Trails of pebbles and breadcrumbs.
2. The old woman and her gingerbread house.
3. Hansel in a cage.

4. Gretel shoves the old woman into the oven.

5. Nature leads them home.

Notice that this story resolves when Gretel preemptively shoves the old woman (often portrayed as a witch) into an oven. Here the consequences of that resolution reveal a theme that is both attractive and misleading. Having become hopelessly lost, the two children shouldn't be permitted, in storytelling terms, to simply run home. (Otherwise, why were they lost in the first place?) Nor are they rescued by some deus ex machina mechanism such as the arrival of a friendly woodcutter. Instead, they are saved by their own virtue. At the end of *Hansel and Gretel*, they find themselves separated from the way home by a river. A duck responds to their request for safe passage by ferrying them across, presumably because nature recognizes their innocence. Still children, their affinity with creation is untrammeled. The theme is thus something like: *Violence is compatible with virtue.*

Again, these are approximations. The point is that however we state the class of experience explored in the resolution of this story, we arrive at a contradiction. We're being told a pleasant and attractive lie. That self-defense may sometimes be necessary is not in question. But does such action really leave a person in a state of innocence? Hansel has been caged, and Gretel has killed an old woman. Could such children really escape morally and psychologically unscathed?

Some have even pointed out that *Hansel and Gretel* is a terrible foreshadowing of the Holocaust. "That the witch is often represented as a figure with stereotypical Jewish traits," Maria Tatar writes, "makes this [oven] scene all the more ominous."[9] Though my own objection to the story is not based on such historical hindsight, I do think the lie at its heart is closely tied to those that fueled the Nazi death camps.

At any rate, stories carry enormous power to shape human development and influence culture. They exist to preserve and communicate meaning—specifically the meaning of life. They utilize basic elements that nearly everyone recognizes (characterization, plot, context, theme, and voice), even as they depend upon and promote shared moral values within a community.

This is why Christians ought to be story specialists. Not only do we have the best story, we have the best reasons for telling it. As Leonard Sweet and Michael Adam Beck put it, "The story of that One is the story of us all. The story of the Incarnate One is the story of us, incarnations all. The story of the Son of God is the story of every son and daughter of God."[10]

Entering the Great Pyramid

Understanding how story works will not only bring new light to the Bible, it will illuminate every area of life. We are wired for story because it is how we recognize the divine patterns around us. God is telling his story not just through the Scriptures but through all of creation. Through life—the good, the bad, and the perplexing. Indeed, he is telling it through us.

Eugene Peterson writes, "Story isn't imposed on our lives; it invites us into its life. As we enter and imaginatively participate, we find ourselves in a more spacious, freer, and more coherent world. We didn't know all this was going on! We had never noticed all this significance!"[11] But as James Bryan Smith points out in *The Magnificent Story*, there is yet another reason the church must restore our storied past and learn to present the gospel as a story for the present. It's not just story in general we were designed to enter, but one particular story. Smith says, "We were made not just to enjoy stories but to enter them. We long to take our lives, our stories, and merge them with another story. This is truly what we long for. But we desire more than a children's bedtime story. We were made for something much bigger."[12]

We were made to live inside the grand story pattern revealed in the entire arc of the Bible from Genesis to Revelation. "You can't escape living in and through a story," Leonard Sweet writes. "All of us are living a story. The question is what story and whose story are you living? Madison Avenue? Wall Street? Hollywood? Or Bethlehem?"[13]

We were made to enter the story of Christ, the one true story, and so follow in his footsteps: from desert to valley to mountain; from garden to cross to resurrection; from life to death and back again to life.

His story—the story of Jesus—is the only story worth living. It is the Great Pyramid of our faith.

2

THE STORYTELLER'S PARABLE

In graduate school I signed up for a class called Introduction to Old English. Old English in this case was not merely olde, but *eald Englisc*—a linguistic relic that predates Chaucer and Shakespeare.

Most of this dead language's surviving documents are pieces of the New Testament that were originally hand-copied by monks. Our class homework was typically to translate some very Germanic-looking passage from the Gospels into modern English. As a new Christian, I found this process both tedious and fascinating. I eventually dropped the class, but for the few weeks I was enrolled I did feel a strange connection to history through the text.

One class period we spent most of our time reading through Mark 4:1–25. This part of Mark's Gospel focuses on the parable of the sower and its explanation, as well as a short passage the NIV labels "A Lamp on a Stand."

At the end of the translation process, a student asked, "Birds? Soil? Roots? What does this *mean*?"

We were seated around the outside of a square of tables and facing the center, so we could all see each other's faces. I remember thinking that several people looked very confused.

The professor, who sat to my immediate left, pointed not at me but at the student to my right. "What do *you* think it means?" he asked.

"Oh, I don't know."

"And you?" the professor asked of the next student. "What do *you* think it means?"

"I don't really know either."

One by one he went around the room, pointing and asking the same question of every student except me. I'm introverted enough that I didn't really mind, but after a dozen or so clueless responses I was fascinated.

We had just read not only the parable but Christ's explanation of what it meant. How could anyone in the room *not* know its meaning? We had just translated a very clear explanation of a very simple concept. The seed was the Word, the sower was Jesus, the four types of soil were four conditions of the human heart that responded to him in four different ways. It wasn't difficult.

Was it?

After the professor asked the last student (though still not me) and received a final baffled shrug, the student who had first raised her hand said again, "So what *does* it mean?"

Our teacher shook his head. "I have no idea."

This got a laugh from the class, but I couldn't stop thinking about it. Was it possible I had just witnessed the parable playing itself out in a college classroom, the "birds of the air" snatching away understanding in spite of the fact the clear meaning of the story lay written out in modern English right in front of us—in our own handwriting?

To really understand what's going on in Mark 4, it is helpful to picture the way this story must have played out when Jesus originally told it. Put yourself in the place of a local, someone from Capernaum who has heard rumors of strange healings and even stranger teachings.

A holy man who works on the Sabbath? A rabbi who takes students from the ranks of fishermen and zealots and tax collectors? A human who commands demons and denounces the temple elders?

Who wouldn't want to hear from such a man, if only as an oddity?

So you trudge down the coast of the Sea of Galilee and gather with the crowd that has collected in the cove. Maybe you played here as a child and recall shouting "Hellooo!" at the half-bowl of sloping earth just to hear your own voice's effortless rebound.

Here there is plenty of room, and you won't need to get your feet wet in order to catch the master's words. The rabbi—Jesus of Nazareth—has already pushed off from shore and is steadying himself on the raised stern as two fishermen lift their dripping oars from the water. The thump of wet wood against dry is strangely magnified, almost an introduction, and the voices of those around you subside. For just a moment there's only the sound of the lapping waves.

"Listen!" the rabbi says at last—as if anyone were *not* listening. "A farmer went out to sow his seed. As he was scattering the seed, some fell along the path, and the birds came and ate it up."

A farmer? Seed? Birds? So he is telling a story, yes? But not one from the Scriptures. At least, not a story you've ever heard before. And does the farmer have a name?

"Some fell on rocky places," this Jesus fellow continues, "where it did not have much soil. It sprang up quickly, because the soil was shallow. But when the sun came up, the plants were scorched, and they withered because they had no root. Other seed fell among thorns, which grew up and choked the plants, so that they did not bear grain."

You may not be a farmer, but this is no surprise. Everyone knows that bad soil means a bad crop. *Sounds like this farmer doesn't know his own business!*

"Still other seed," the rabbi says, one hand cupped over his eyes, "fell on good soil. It came up, grew and produced a crop, multiplying thirty, sixty, or even a hundred times."

He stares out at the crowd for a long moment as if waiting for a response. Instead there is just silence—the crowd waiting him out.

"He who has ears to hear, let him hear," he says and sits down.

A few minutes later a handful of young men—his disciples, presumably—splash out in the shallow waters to stand waist deep around the boat. They are talking, but with their voices too low to be heard.

It's a long time before Jesus stands again to speak, and this time the story is about weeds planted by a farmer's enemy. And something about a mustard tree and a woman mixing yeast into dough. Then he motions to the two men with oars and they maneuver the boat back to shore and the rabbi heads into town, trailing curiosity.

You shrug at a man who holds his hands out palms up, as if begging for answers. "Why look at me?" you ask. "Do I look like a rabbi?"

The cove is filled with the sound of lapping waves and the play of sunlight on water as you turn back toward Capernaum. *What was that? What did it mean? Did I miss something? Surely there must be more!*

A Lamp on a Stand

There is more, of course, but only the disciples—those who got wet crowding the boat—were privy to the meaning of these parables.

This fact is particularly challenging when we read how Jesus unpacked the meaning of the parable of the sower. His explanations are sometimes as loaded with implication as the stories he's unpacking.

When asked why he speaks in parables, he gives a long answer that (1) points to the new covenant; (2) references a contextually ironic verse from Isaiah; (3) explains the parallels of the sower story with almost childlike simplicity; (4) adds a question in the form of a metaphor that both invites and obfuscates; and (5) commands a response with conditions for both acceptance and rejection.

None of this is what we expect, and all of it is consistently misunderstood. As Leonard Sweet points out, "The church's failure to tell stories in a culture that talks in stories is a story in and of itself."[1]

Our lack of story fluency has made it difficult for us to glean contextual significance from the parables, and our oversimplification of the New Testament has made it hard for us to see that the new covenant is about more than forgiveness. It is also about God teaching us personally—God to human, Spirit to flesh—by writing his law on our hearts and minds (Heb. 8:10–11). But *how* he does that is even more unexpected than the fact that he's willing to do it.

The parable of the sower wasn't meant to be understood quickly or easily. It wasn't meant to be interpreted solely through the use of human reason. It was designed to require a dialogue between storyteller and audience. "The secret of the kingdom of God has been given to you," Jesus told his disciples in Mark 4:11. "But to those on the outside . . ." This is an either-or situation. You either have access to the secret of the kingdom or you are outside the kingdom. Anyone who wants to know what the parable means must either ask God about it or remain puzzled. There is no third option. There is no figuring it out. No one understands it on their own. And as Jesus asks in verse 13, if you do not understand the parable of the sower, how will you understand any of his parables?

This doesn't mean that the parable has no effect on those outside. On the contrary, the point of speaking in parables is that it provokes curiosity while respecting and affirming self-determination. When Jesus quotes Isaiah, he isn't pronouncing judgment but holding up a mirror to the human heart, so that "they may be ever seeing but never perceiving, and ever hearing but never understanding; otherwise they might turn and be forgiven!" (Mark 4:12).

Your spiritual condition determines how you respond. The parable simply provides an exit door for those unwilling to take the ride. Those on the outside are allowed to misunderstand if they prefer ignorance to repentance. They *may* (not must) see but not perceive. They *may* (not must) hear but not understand. They're allowed to close their minds as they have closed their hearts.

The field is full of Easter eggs and Christ has posted a sign: FREE FOR THE ASKING! But you must ask. He will not drag you into the field. Nor will you find the eggs without his help—even if you care to look.

But if you ask, there's no end to the colorful treasure you will receive. And when you receive it, you'll be shocked at how clear and obvious it suddenly seems: "The farmer sows the word. Some people are like seed along the path, where the word is sown. As soon as they hear it, Satan comes and takes away the word that was sown in them" (Mark 4:14–15).

Why then does Jesus speak in parables?

It's important we not assume that we now have the answer. Even after explaining the entire parable, Jesus isn't done answering this question.

Why do I speak in parables? For the same reason you put a lamp on a stand.

The metaphor of the lampstand in Mark 4:21–23 is deeply connected to everything that's happening between Jesus and the disciples; it's the ultimate answer to their question, and one we have yet to fully recognize. Instead of a simple answer, Jesus responds with a simple question: Why do you put a lamp on a stand?

Answer: to make its light go farther.

The parable isn't the message; it's the mechanism. It's not the lamp; it's the stand. The *explanation* Jesus gave to his disciples is the lamp. The parable everyone heard is a way of magnifying his light.

We Are Story Thinkers

Movie theaters operate on this principle. House lights are placed high on the walls or in the ceiling. Those safety lights that illuminate the aisles are always fixed a foot or two off the floor.

On a trip to Haiti, I once stayed in a house on the side of a mountain. One morning before sunrise, I looked across the valley behind the house and saw a tiny light bobbing along in the black silhouette of the far peak. When I asked what the light was, my host replied that it was a single candle held aloft by an old woman walking to market miles away.

This is counterintuitive to anyone enmeshed in church tradition. We're used to the assumption that clarity of message is the pinnacle of both expository preaching and storytelling. Nothing warms our hearts like an old-fashioned sermon punctuated in bullet points. More than one theologian has bemoaned this ecclesiastical quirk. Leonard Sweet, no stranger to the pulpit, writes, "When a church is fed only points and propositions, rules and answers, it's like a body nourished on husks and shells. Without propositions, it's like trying to stand up without a skeleton . . . but propositions and principles come from the stories, not stories from the propositions."[2]

An unbiased review of the methods Jesus used during his earthly ministry should make us question our propositional paradigms. The church isn't using Jesus's approach but its opposite. We read what he did and then go and do otherwise. Both our tract-based, "Four Spiritual Laws" approach to evangelism and our deductive, catechismal sermons expressly rely on a method Christ compared to putting one's light under a bushel. Deductive sermons don't make the light go farther; they snuff it out.

Jesus rarely explained himself to anyone except his disciples. To everyone else, he told weird stories that didn't make sense and weren't packaged with a summarizing explanation. To those who weren't sold-out followers, to those who simply went through the motions, he spoke in riddles and puzzles and parallel narratives.

Even the Sermon on the Mount, which begins with a series of general statements and proceeds through a list of moral laws, relies heavily on short parables and metaphors that strain our powers of deduction to the breaking point—and then ends in a story. This sermon, the height of Christ's expository preaching, overflows with Old Testament references and real-life implications left open to interpretation: *You are salt. Cut off your hand. Do not announce it with trumpets. Store up treasures in heaven. The eye is the lamp of the body. Consider the lilies. First take the plank out of your own eye. Knock and the door will be opened. Enter through the narrow gate. They are wolves in sheep's clothing.*

Not only did Jesus speak in parables to his followers, he spoke this way to his friends. Even his inner circle rarely got an explanation unless they asked for one.

This characteristic of Jesus's discipleship is so foreign to our way of thinking that we don't recognize it in the Gospels, though it's clear as tap water when we read them as stories.

The principle is this: to make any message go farther, reach more people, last longer in their minds, and do more good in terms of changing their modes of thinking and their behavior, you must communicate in their native language. And in every culture from the dawn of creation, that language, for humans, is not logic but story. "Stories are what made the past, and stories are what will make the future. . . . How do you navigate a world of constant turbulence, negotiate cascading avalanches of information and chicanes of alternative facts and fake news? You use the GPS of narrative."[3]

In a 2019 interview with tech guru Lex Fridman, Elon Musk, the modern embodiment of Iron Man, gave a fascinating justification for hardwiring supercomputers to the human brain. Musk's Neuralink corporation aims to provide real-time thought-mapping that will make integrated artificial intelligence a reality in the near future, in part because, according to Musk, we have no hope of matching the digital intelligences that are coming, so why not join them? Here's how he explains the human brain:

> We've got a monkey brain with a computer stuck on it. That's the human brain. And a lot of our impulses are driven by the monkey brain. And the computer, the cortex, is constantly trying to make the monkey brain happy. It's not the cortex that's steering the monkey brain; it's the monkey brain steering the cortex. . . . It seems like, surely the really smart thing should control the dumb thing, but actually the dumb thing controls the smart thing.[4]

As offensive as this statement may seem, it aligns with Paul's view of human nature: "The mind governed by the flesh is death, but the mind governed by the Spirit is life and peace" (Rom. 8:6). But where Musk offers no escape from the tyranny of the monkey brain, Paul suggests there's a force powerful enough to wrestle away control of the cortex from the limbic system. One might say that the cortex controlled by the monkey brain is death, but the cortex controlled by the Spirit is life and peace. But however you phrase it, the point is that your mind isn't actually in control. It is being controlled, either by your limbic system—that is, your emotions and desires for food, sex, sleep, and comfort—or by the Spirit of God.

We aren't driven by reason. We're driven by emotion and metaphor and, in our best moments, by spiritual desperation—all of which are the domain of story.

This is why it's largely ineffective to build evangelistic and liturgical practices on the illusion of clear thinking. We aren't clear thinkers, even in our best moments. We are story thinkers, which is something profoundly different. In his book *The Gospel According to Starbucks*, Leonard Sweet writes,

> The power of the Word to move people from rote-religion to full-life immersion is not in the words themselves. It's in the images, the stories, the music of Scripture. . . . Since the mind is made of metaphors (remember, we dream in pictures, not text), the greatest power over others is the power held by those who choose the metaphors.[5]

We are driven by moving metaphors: the stories we hear, the stories we identify with, and, most of all, the stories we choose to live. We derive our identity from story. But life-giving stories are rarely clear. Instead, the stories that truly shape us are the ones that mirror our earthy, sweat-stained approximations of truth we call life experience.

We are shaped by pyramid stories.

Deductive Doing

Journalists sometimes refer to stories as being shaped either as pyramids or upside-down pyramids.

Hard news stories use an inverted pyramid structure. They begin with the basic details of a story—who, what, when, where, why, how—and work toward greater specificity as the story unfolds. First we learn that the *Hindenburg* airship exploded on May 6, 1937, while attempting to land at Lakehurst Naval Air Station in New Jersey. Later we're given details about the presumed cause of the explosion, and only near the end do specific quotes from witnesses appear. The story begins with an overview and ends with a small fragment of the bigger picture. Such news is considered *deductive* because it works from general narration to specific details.

Inverted pyramid structure isn't just the preferred structure of journalists. It's also favored by preachers and professors and propagandists. Why? Because a deductive format allows the storyteller to select whatever evidence or proof is needed to support their main point. This is how news stories are slanted—with carefully selected facts. Propaganda is built on facts, not lies.

This is also the main reason college writing courses tend to focus on the five paragraph essay. An introduction followed by three increasingly powerful proofs and a conclusion is simple but effective training in the power of deductive persuasion. Rather than making us more aware of how such stories can be twisted, however, these assignments may only strengthen our perception that deductive storytelling is normal or that all storytelling is deductive.

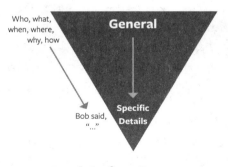

Deductive Structure

All is clearly stated:
Hard News, Propaganda, Lectures, Speeches

Brian Anse Patrick explains how inverted pyramids are used in journalism:

> In practice, the story content is selected to fit the lead rather than the other way around. It is a style or recipe that lends itself to industrial hack writing, which is a dietary staple both in propaganda and journalism. That many prominent propagandists have risen up from the ranks of journalists attests to the indispensability of the news format in controlling the flow of information.[6]

It's one thing to say that Baghdad Bob selected his content to fit his leads. It's perhaps not much different to say that CNN or the *New York Times* does it too. But preachers?

Rather than present a deductive list of proofs that American evangelical services are dominated by inverted pyramid sermons, I will defer instead to the reader's personal experience and a single quote from a theologian. Last time you were at church, was the sermon essentially bullet points proving a clearly articulated concept from the Bible? Were you, perhaps, the one preaching it? (And if you were, would your seminary professors have approved?) Leonard Sweet writes, "A deductive sermon appeals to the mind but not the heart. It expresses faith not in felt terms or felt needs but in nuggets for the noggin."[7]

In short, we may be so indoctrinated in the dogma of deduction that we have trouble seeing this sort of reasoning as unreasonable. We certainly don't imagine that deductive storytelling is a *problem*.

Inductive Inspiring

The alternative is more complicated than flipping our story pyramids over so that they are no longer balancing on a single point. Still, moving from deductive to inductive is a good place to start.

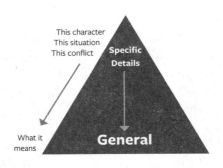

Inductive Structure

Specifics lead to generalities:
Features, Fables, Morality Tales

The inductive, right-side-up pyramid structure is useful because it begins with specifics and moves toward the general. This is how we live life. We don't begin in the realm of general principles—for example, "Never steal." Rather, we begin in the particularities of here and now, the soil and sky and sandwiches of daily experience where *this moment I am hungry and no one is looking and what's the big deal, anyway?* Eventually such experiences, and their consequences, may lead to a resolution that one should never steal.

Aesop's fables are examples of inductive, pyramidal stories. They begin with specific if fanciful situations and conclude with a clearly stated moral. After the fox fails to secure a delicious-looking bunch of grapes, he concludes that they're probably sour anyway and walks away. The storyteller then tells us the moral: *It is easy to despise what you cannot have.*

This is a well-known story. But does its last line seem a bit on the nose? A touch patronizing or even preachy?

Such stories tend to be short—more anecdotes than stories—for exactly this reason. A brief illustration can make the message or moral easier to understand and more entertaining, but a long story implicitly promises something besides an easy, microwave interpretation. This is probably one reason Jesus kept his inductive parables short, like when he said, "No one can serve two masters. Either he will hate the one and love the other, or he will be devoted to the one and despise the other. You cannot serve both God and money" (Matt. 6:24).

Inductive storytelling is flawed because, though it more closely resembles how we process life than does deductive storytelling, it departs from reality by arriving at the conclusion for us. Rather than inviting the audience to search for the moral or general principle hidden in the events of the story, an inductive story hits us between the eyes with it. Unlike in life, an inductively presented moral can't be missed.

Here again is a story problem we often fail to understand. If experience is the best teacher, the best way a story can teach me anything is to allow me to process its conclusion for myself. Were I teaching a boy how to drive nails, I could tell him a dozen times that he was holding the nail wrong. But he probably won't learn the lesson until he bangs a finger.

In the church, our stories sometimes try to apply this principle, but since we don't trust the audience to arrive at acceptable conclusions, we tend to package the truth, Aesop-style, inside an obvious concluding moral. At best we ask the audience to hold out their fingers for an instructive bashing. Whatever we end up hitting, it isn't their fingers.

The Silent Exclamation

Great storytellers don't apply the hammer themselves. They give the hammer and the nail to the audience and wait for the inevitable. Why?

Because in life the general principle is never precisely known in the moment. Instead, it is inferred from details that point to a *most likely* explanation. When you hear rumors at the office, you draw conclusions based on what you know about those passing along information. When you try to help a child through some troubling phase, you draw conclusions based on their history, habits, and personality. When you sense a friendship is growing cold, you may retrace your past interactions in your memory looking for clues about what caused the rift.

Life isn't packaged into neat containers. It doesn't come to us labeled with biblical references and Socratic virtues. These are only ever understood contextually. Which means that we arrive at them through an *abductive* process.

Abductive storytelling begins in the specific and ends just short of the general. It invites an audience to hypothesize some principle that is never directly stated. Like the Great Pyramid at Giza, its base is concealed and its inner chamber is hidden. Any concluding exclamation is utterly silent.

Because its limits mirror those we encounter in life, it has enormous power to move. It doesn't just entertain. It conceals, preserves, and reveals layers of meaning that are not apparent on the surface. But because it never arrives at a clear, synthesizing general principle, an abductive story risks being misunderstood, just as Jesus risked being misunderstood when he told parables to crowds who would never hear his detailed explanations.

Abductive Structure

Specifics lead to implications:
Parables, Novels, Movies

51

As lampstands, the long-form parables of Jesus are uniquely abductive. "For whatever is hidden is meant to be disclosed, and whatever is concealed is meant to be brought out into the open" (Mark 4:22).

His stories are rich with hidden meaning that was intended to be understood. But understanding comes with a price. The hidden things will be *disclosed*, not discovered. Insight is available but must be sought. True revelation must be received. Furthermore, we aren't just invited to ponder their deeper significance over time; we're commanded to consider carefully what we hear. For with the measure we use—teaspoon, trowel, or truck—it will be measured back to us (Mark 4:24).

Consider Carefully What You Hear

In the remainder of this book we'll consider carefully the story of the Bible, which is really the story of Jesus, using the measure of story. Theme, context, characterization, voice, and plot will be our egg detectors and our treasure chests. There is, however, one condition upon which this sort of exploration depends.

In his groundbreaking book on post-critical theory, Michael Polanyi writes, "Only a Christian who stands in the service of his faith can understand Christian theology and only he can enter into the religious meaning of the Bible."[8] The price of admission isn't mastery of the English language or even of the language of story but a willingness to leave behind any modern notions of personal objectivity. None of us stands above the fray. To enter God's story one must be willing to enter it fully and on its own terms. To find a place in the story of Jesus we must have the humility to submit to it.

Biblical scholarship is heavily dominated by a critical approach that assumes a distanced, 10,000-foot view far above the text. Faith thus becomes an object of scrutiny rather than a lens through which Scripture is interpreted. This position shapes the sorts of theories and explanations scholars entertain as plausible. For instance, some scholars have assumed that repeated plot points indicate scribal error rather than deliberate narrative or structural meaning.

In order to understand the story, we must let it function as a story. We must begin by assuming that everything in the text is meaningful. This is especially true when viewing the Old Testament as an extended typological and metaphorical story arc that foreshadows the incarnate life of Christ. You cannot see Christ in the Old Testament if you won't see him in the New Testament. And you won't see him in the New Testament if your Old Testament is nothing more than a collection of interesting myths and scribal errors (Luke 16:31).

It is true that I begin with a bias—but so does the scholar-skeptic. I cannot escape the fact of my own faith, nor do I want to. I believe the story as written—in part because Jesus believed it. I accept as a starting place a Jesus hermeneutic that begins with his statement "the Scripture cannot be set aside" (John 10:35).

Those who approach the Bible from a position of skepticism are equally inhibited. Unbelief doesn't make one objective. And if mere observation can affect the outcome in quantum physics, why is it difficult to believe that our starting assumptions may steer what we see in the Scriptures? "No one can see the kingdom of God unless they are born again" (John 3:3).

The skeptic and the believer both begin subjectively. I'm willing to admit my subjective starting point and its difficulties. I approach this particular mountain from the west. The skeptic attacks it from the east. Neither of us is favored with a bird's-eye view. I merely say that this mountain was created to be climbed, and climbed from the west. If you scale the other side you miss the truly spectacular views. The Bible was written as a religious text to a community of believers. In order to be understood fully it must be read in that light.

What follows is my attempt to throw off the limiting paradigms of five hundred years of textual vivisection in order to see the Bible as a story—as *the* story of both humanity and God—using the five common story elements nearly everyone understands.

THEME

3

THE BEST THEME PARK EVER

If you ask someone what a movie or book is about, you're likely to hear a synopsis of its plot. But a story's plot isn't what a story is *about*. That role belongs to its theme. Stories use character arcs and turning points and the dramatic tension of disasters and dilemmas to create classes of experience that speak to us of reality. Those things are part of the language of story. But they are *how* the story speaks, not *what* the story speaks.

According to Leland Ryken,

> A good story does, indeed, entertain us, and it embodies human experience in such a way as to lead us to relive it along with the characters in the story. But a story is also intended by the author to convey a message. Further, this message can at some point be formulated as ideas. The literary term for such ideas is *themes* (generalizations about life).[1]

His definition of theme as a *generalization about life* is useful, and even though it's an oversimplification to say that every

57

story can be reduced to a quantifiable summary or formula about life, yet there is some truth in this. The danger here lies in our tendency to equate formula with solution, to mistake a map for the roadways it represents.

I know the basic ingredients of the finest wines in the world; my father was an amateur winemaker, and to this day I can vividly recall the aromas of that process. But I don't have the actual wines—neither my father's nor those of, say, Albert Bichot. It isn't enough to have the formula. One must also have what is tangible and tasteable. Without something to swirl in a glass, in other words, what good is a list of ingredients? A theme extracted from its story has no persuasive power.

Nevertheless, themes are sometimes worth extracting, either for the sake of learning how stories work or, more practical still, for the sake of putting into words what you have already understood a different way. Ryken asserts, "The best art always allows us to come in, to see something of ourselves that we would not be able to see or know otherwise."[2]

Napoleon couldn't put into words what he experienced in the King's Chamber of the Great Pyramid of Giza, and something was lost to history. Perhaps he couldn't put into words what he experienced because he didn't have the requisite humility for true revelation, and his time in the heart of that wondrous mountain was the sort of experience had by anyone who dismisses a truth they are not ready for.

Maybe Napoleon would have understood better what he encountered at Giza had he gone there after his defeat at Waterloo.

Theme Park

Many accomplished storytellers who have written about the nature of narrative art say two compatible but not necessarily intuitive things about it. First, they say that stories can't be reduced to a simple formula, and second, that stories tend to work by embodying ideals or values in the actions of their characters. In *Les Misérables*, for instance, the clash between Inspector Javert and ex-criminal Jean Valjean demonstrates the subtleties of the timeless conflict between judgment and mercy. *Romeo and Juliet* is a kind of dramatized argument in which Shakespeare shows us the destructive power of tribal hatred and the one principle—love—that is strong enough to dispel it. In *A Christmas Carol*, Charles Dickens depicts the unraveling of Scrooge's self-absorption through the revelatory visitations of four spirits, and in so doing convinces us of a theme that is easy to accept but hard to live: *the business of every life is the welfare of others*. Even James Barrie's classic children's tale, *Peter Pan*, tells a profound but difficult truth through the action of its whimsical plot, namely, *innocence is heartless*.

But the reduction of any given story into its corresponding embedded generalizations about life isn't the most important or interesting thing about the story element we call theme. What matters here is that we take these thematic generalizations, based as they are on a universal moral compass of ideals, to be true without recognizing where they come from or what they themselves are pointing to.

Stories work best when their meaning derives from the action and characters of their events. Lessons that are tacked on as moral finger-wagging will be disregarded by the audience. Even when those expository sermons embedded oh-so-cleverly in a character's dialogue are agreeable to us, we aren't changed by them. We don't value meaning that we don't arrive at ourselves. If you don't go through the emotional and intellectual work of dissecting a story in your own mind, if you don't put the pieces together yourself, you won't internalize what it's teaching you.

This is why ideals have so much power not just to make us feel deep emotions but to influence us for better or worse. Love and hatred and responsibility and revenge and honesty and greed are part of the grammar of story because they're so interwoven into our real lives that we take them for granted. We won't all agree on the fine points of religion, but we do mostly agree about what honesty or selfishness or courage is. In other words, ideals are self-evident, and because they are self-evident, they're almost universally understood. They serve as a bridge between storyteller and audience.

Aristotle saw virtues as existing in the place of balance between excess and deficiency; extravagant modesty, for instance, might really be a form of attention-seeking. A more refined approach to the virtues is perhaps the one accepted by both Greek and Christian thinkers, what are sometimes referred to as the cardinal virtues: prudence, temperance, justice, and courage.[3] The theological virtues of faith, hope, and love are derived directly from the Bible, and yet they are widely accepted as virtues in stories when embodied subtly in the actions of the characters.

Whatever our basis for the ideals or virtues, humans use them in the interpretation of stories. Nor is it necessary to define precisely what these virtues are for an audience to be motivated and persuaded through their use. We all seem to have a moral compass, whatever that represents, and it's accessible to the storyteller in service of dramatic art.

Would Dinosaurs Eat People?

Consider Michael Crichton's *Jurassic Park*. The novel's thematic clash is unusual in that it pits chaos versus control. In the story, humans have figured out how to re-create dinosaurs by retrieving their DNA found in prehistoric mosquitoes embedded in amber. This power—the power to restore life and use it for the amusement of tourists and the making of wealth—is contrasted against a subtle but pervasive feeling that something about this process is wrong. When reading the book, I want to go to Jurassic Park as a tourist and see living sauropods and velociraptors and triceratops for myself. The sense of wonder at human ingenuity and the grandeur of nature is palpable. At the same time, I cannot escape the tension inherent in the premise: What can go wrong probably will go wrong—and then what?

Chaos and *control* are the key words, but as ideals they are really stand-ins for humility and arrogance. Over and over, Hammond and his scientists assert their domination, their ability to control nature and prevent the sort of unexpected consequences that have accompanied advances in technology down through history. Jurassic Park is an island, so the dinosaurs can't escape; everything that goes in or out of Isla Nublar is strictly controlled. Moreover, the animals are kept in high-tech pens made of steel and concrete. These walls are topped with electrified fences. The power grid has redundant backups in case of storm or other calamity. Nor can the animals reproduce naturally, for they have all been created female. The dinosaur population is tracked by computer, and just in case anything should go wrong in spite of all these controls, the island has its own world-class hunter who is capable of locating and eliminating any nasty surprises.

Furthermore, Crichton is always two steps ahead of us, answering our questions well before we think to ask them and pointing out that the park is extremely *safe* because it is extremely *controlled*. Nothing has escaped InGen's attention to detail.

At the same time, all this control makes us uneasy because we can't help but associate it with arrogance. We know in our bones that Ian Malcolm, the chaos theorist, is right to warn Hammond and the others that they can never think of everything; chaos will break down the illusion of control and expose the hubris latent in the whole project.

The theme of *Jurassic Park* is therefore that *humanity cannot control nature.*

The IDEALS of
Jurassic Park

Children	Scientists	Hammond	Jurassic Park
Humility	False Humility	Arrogance	Arrogance destroys itself.
Control	Loss of Control	Chaos	Chaos masquerades as control.

I	II	III

Yes, I understand that it's a story about dinosaurs eating people. But Michael Crichton didn't write the book to say, "Dinosaurs would eat people if they got the chance." He wrote it to say, "The *reason* dinosaurs would eat people if they got the chance is that humans cannot control nature."

At heart, *Jurassic Park* is a validation of humility, a way to reinforce in us a respect for nature and a realistic understanding of our place within it.

Story's Moral Compass

In the language of story, moral absolutes are called ideals. In stories, an ideal is any standard of perfection such as love, forgiveness, revenge, honesty, or cruelty. Not necessarily *good* things, but things that are absolute.

No story can work if the storyteller can't point to something like forgiveness and make it the hinge point of the protagonist's moral journey. Without ideals, without a clear set of moral parameters, there's no basis for a character arc. Without a clear character arc, there's no change, and without change there's no story.

Imagine a giant nautical compass, something large enough to be segmented into hundreds of radial degrees. Remember that a true compass can point in all directions but is only trustworthy because there is such a thing as true north. In this case, true north would represent the idea that some ideals are positive and others negative. Forgiveness is positive, and revenge, its diametric opposite, is negative.

This doesn't mean we all agree about what's moral and what's immoral. Nor does it mean storytellers can't try to influence an audience's perception of the moral compass. On the contrary, contemporary novels and films often try to undermine traditional values in the name of artistic expression.

In the previous sentence, two sets of moral ideals are pitted against each other: *traditional values* versus *artistic expression.* Or perhaps *tradition* versus *art*, or even *values* versus *expression.* How you see that argument may be a function of your political beliefs or your upbringing or even your selfish preferences. But however you see it, you're siding with one of the two absolutes.

When storytellers try to shape an audience's moral compass, they never abandon the security of moral absolutes. They can't abandon them, because if they did, their stories would cease to function as stories.

The movie *The Cider House Rules* is a great illustration of this. Protagonist Homer Wells is a young man being raised—and tutored—by an abortionist in a WWII-era orphanage. In part because of his distaste for abortions, Homer eventually leaves the security of the orphanage to work at an apple orchard. In the film's climactic moral dilemma, Homer, now come of age, relents and agrees to abort the baby of a woman raped by her own father. *Cider House* is a brilliantly written, well-acted, well-constructed, gorgeously filmed story that tries to convince the audience in a very subtle way that Satanism is true.

I'm not using the word *Satanism* for its shock value, like Dana Carvey's character the Church Lady in old *Saturday Night Live* skits. I'm simply pointing out that the theme of this film is that all moral absolutes are illusions and the source of our moral judgment resides exclusively in ourselves. That is the essence of modern Satanism, and its connection to the film isn't accidental. Consider the story's essential imagery of apples being pulped en masse.

What makes *Cider House* worthy of mention here is its revelation of the moral compass as inescapable: the story uses a moral absolute (rape is always wrong) in order to prove to the audience that moral absolutes don't exist. Apparently even moral relativists are driven by moral absolutes.

On a deeper level, this is the language of story expressing its true nature. Not that moral relativism is wrong (it is), but that story rejects the premise of moral relativism in the same way physics rejects the model of a steady-state universe. If I try to frame a story around the premise that moral absolutes don't exist, I will only end up with something unrecognizable as a story.

Whatever the moral compass represents, it cannot be bypassed in the service of story. The compass is an essential and foundational part of narrative structure—probably because it is essential to our humanity.

The Compass Is Perfect

For story to work as it does, this compass of charged ideals must have three recognizable traits. It must be:

1. Perfect
2. Comprehensible
3. Uncompromising

The compass is perfect in that it exists across every spectrum of human experience and morality; it contains every conceivable ideal, from honesty to courage to desire. It is perfect in the sense that a yardstick can be precise down to the smallest of measurements. Furthermore, it accounts for a spectrum of positive and negative values that are themselves perfect and pure, though not always good. In other words, it sets up love as a perfect ideal, and also hatred. It marks out joy, and also sorrow. Polar opposites are as necessary to the moral compass of story as they are to earth's magnetic field.

Notice that the moral compass as I'm describing it accounts for even the tiniest of moral flaws. It's also preloaded with ideals that result from our interaction with the compass itself. It doesn't just point to the ideals we might expect: *love* and *honesty* and *courage*. It also seems to account for the possibility of failure and reversal. That is, some of the points on the compass are marked *forgiveness* and *repentance* and *mercy*. These are ideals that indicate change and growth, without which a story would be impossible. In other words, story's ideals allow for people to become better moral agents.

And that means the moral compass must be comprehensible. If it weren't, we'd have no knowledge of our own moral failures and there would be no reference point, no sense in referring to a compass at all. Our stories wouldn't be moral nor would they call us to change and grow.

And that in turn indicates a third thing, that the moral compass is uncompromising. It is always the human who needs to change, not the compass. *Cider House Rules* notwithstanding, states of perfection do not evolve. Ideals are useful because they're perfect, just as a yardstick is useful because it's always exactly the same length.

To be clear, the moral compass embedded in the language of story may be an artifact of something else, some other human attribute that falls outside the scope of this book. The point is not that moral absolutes are absolute proof of God but that without a moral compass the language of story is meaningless. Every character arc from Beowulf to the latest Disney princess points to the existence of real moral absolutes that do not and cannot change without disappearing altogether.

Like it or not, story is telling us that we're aware of something outside ourselves to which we are all accountable and to which our own behavior is not measuring up.

Principle Versus Power

Story themes are not just generalizations about life. They're arguments about which side of the ideal scale, positive or negative, is better. And not just better but more powerful and more likely to prevail in real life.

Now, the astonishing thing about the language of story is that, from the standpoint of theme, stories almost always side with the ideal that *doesn't* win in real life—or doesn't seem to. After all, in real life do humble people really go further than those who sound their own horn? We pretend they do. But do they really?

Because ideals in stories can be separated into positive and negative sides, it is possible to explore what the ideals found on each side of the compass have in common. How are they actually aligned, and why?

Positive ideals are usually expressed as principles that lack worldly or human power. Love, honesty, and courage are rarely associated with armies or politicians or wealth. On the other hand, negative ideals are often appealing because of their association with the sorts of power that yield immediate gratification. Hatred, lies, revenge, and betrayal are almost always demonstrated in terms of raw power. In *Star Wars*, it's the dark side of the Force that makes power easy. All you have to do is sacrifice your principles.

Seen this way, story's moral compass of ideals is divided into ideals of principle and ideals of power. Which means human stories seem to be telling us—repeatedly and insistently—that principle will always win in the end. In spite of the fact that it often doesn't seem to.

How often has the experience of living taught us the opposite? Don't the powerful usually win in life, at least judging by the short-term outcomes of a single lifespan?

So why does story almost universally take the opposite approach and side with principle? If the point is mere survival, and the main driver of reality is purposeless reproduction, why should honesty be more important than lies, or forgiveness better than revenge?

The first and most obvious answer is that winning through power always comes at a cost. It's a compromise that means short-term success but long-term failure. Sure, Hitler won enormous power through the betrayal of his friends and the seizure of government and the genocide of millions. But he also committed suicide in an underground bunker and is now universally despised. So perhaps story is telling us that it's better to play the long game and look beyond the comfort of our current circumstances. Perhaps story embodies the wisdom of eternity and aims to teach us to live for a better future. After all, you will never have enough power to overcome the sort of power that can be arrayed against you from those who have no principles. Principled power can never be as extreme as its unprincipled counterpart because it will always be limited by the boundaries of virtue. Kidnappers are, in this sense, always more powerful than parents.

A second answer to this question may be that story is trying to tell us principle *should* defeat power, even when it doesn't. The language of story would therefore be based on an ultimate scale rather than a relative one. It would, in fact, be conveying a meaning derived from outside or beyond the mechanistic resources of the material universe. In which case the few rare stories that demonstrate power prevailing over principle exist not to make us power hungry but to make clear the awful consequences of turning, so to speak, to the dark side of the Force.

This implies a third answer, that story *must* allow the negative ideals their place on the stage or the moral compass cannot function as true. The only way a story can prove that the positive ideal is always better than its negative counterpart is for its fences to come down. Every negative must be allowed inside. Any theme park that doesn't allow *all* the ideals to compete is not really a theme park but a playground.

Reality, in other words, is the *only* true theme park. In life you are free to do a good turn to your neighbor just as you are free to do them a bad one. They might even do you a bad turn while you are doing good to them. Moreover, "good" and "bad" are not subjective. They point to ultimate moral standards. Which means that if story is right, then we're living in a world of real ideals, acting out a fantastically complex story that has at its heart a universal theme of principle being opposed by power. Viewed through the lens of story, planet Earth is something like an enormous and complicated set on which the drama of life is spooling out a meaning derived from outside the matter and energy of the cosmos. "All the world's a stage," Shakespeare wrote, "and all the men and women merely players."[4]

Put simply, we are living inside the best theme park ever, even if it isn't always the most fun. This may be harsh, but it's also beautiful. Our world isn't just a place of random events; it's a place of ideals.

How we respond to them is what defines us as humans.

Ubuntu

But there is a fourth reason that story always sides with principle over power, a reason that can summed up in the South African word *ubuntu* (pronounced "oo-BOON-too"), which Oxford Languages defines as "a quality that includes the essential human virtues; compassion and humanity." Ubuntu is identity grounded in relationship. It means "*I* am not *me* without *you.*" As semiotician Crystal Downing puts it, "Personhood is negated without community."[5]

What makes ubuntu relevant here is that it so clearly embodies the unifying basis of all positive ideals. What do love, courage, honesty, compassion, mercy, truth, and humility have in common? Each of them is based in some way on supporting or lifting up the other. Every positive ideal or value depends on relationship. Love is not love without the beloved. Kindness and mercy cannot exist without an object of action. Honesty is impossible without someone who hears the truth. And courage, which so often flows from an allegiance to a larger community, is, as C. S. Lewis pointed out, the virtue that enables every other virtue to withstand testing.[6]

Relationality, ubuntu, is the magnetic north of the moral compass.

We cannot be ourselves apart from someone else, apart from some larger community—a family or clan or tribe or village, however small these may be. Nor can we be ourselves apart from a relationship with our Creator, because it is only in God that we find an external source of meaning. Jean Leclercq writes, "All the virtues are synonymous; whether they are called fear, wisdom, or prudence, they have the same origin and the same end. All are gifts of God; they are directed to eternal life and awaken desire for it."[7]

This is why the negative ideals are all connected by their opposition to the full formation of human identity through relationship. Hatred, selfishness, cowardice, falsehood, and control all place the self above the other. They say, "I don't need you in order to be me. In fact, to be fully me, I need not-you." And this of course is a lie. In sacrificing principle for power one is sacrificing the other for the self. But this sacrifice is really a *destruction* of the self, for you cannot choose the self over the other without erasing your own humanity.

Power without principle is therefore inhuman, but the converse is not true. Principle doesn't need worldly power in order to be human. Principle, in that sense, is divine. It has its origins in God and is a reflection of the heart of God.

What binds the positive ideals together is that they are all expressions of the phrase "God is love." The eternal relationship of Father, Son, and Holy Spirit is the basis of everything meant by the Hebrew word *tov*, which translated means *true* and *beautiful* and *good*. And God has extended that image in and through us.

This is what story is telling us, that *I am not me without you*. And if I'm not me without you, then I cannot sacrifice you without sacrificing myself. I cannot choose power over principle without becoming something less than human, something antithetical to *tov*: something false and ugly and evil.

If the language of story is to be believed, then such a surrender of our humanity would be worse than death, and no amount of temporal power could compensate us for the loss.

4

AN IDEAL WORLD

The first conflict depicted in the Bible is the story of humanity's fall from innocence in the garden of Eden. Tempted by a serpent, the first two people—who had been made in God's image and given dominion over the earth—succumbed to the desire to eat from the one tree they were warned to avoid, the tree of the knowledge of good and evil.

This story has been the subject of so much scrutiny by theologians and philosophers that it's difficult to approach as a story. Yet this first conflict must be understood if we are to recognize the story the Bible is telling, because the fall is where the story begins to look like a story.

However you take it, this is where the biblical drama of history begins. Since story as we know it doesn't exist without conflict of some sort, we can say that here is where the story of humanity became recognizable as a story. The garden of Eden is more than just a mythic container for prehistory. It's the proximate cause of every conflict that followed, and as such it opens the main story arc of Scripture.

Eden is crammed with poetic language, with metaphor, and with multivalent symbolism. Because so much is either implied or deliberately left ambiguous, we can't help but draw conclusions based on our own experiences and cultural values and ways of reading literature. This is why the Eden story is so easy to misread, particularly when scrutinizing it for doctrines or for propositional truths instead of approaching it first as a story. To understand the implications of Eden we must wrestle with the meanings conveyed in the interaction of its various story elements. To really discover what this story is about (and remember, a story is never about its plot), we must recognize its underlying theme.

This, as I've said, is difficult for numerous reasons. But the most important reason is one the story itself points out. We have trouble recognizing the theme here because by the time we're old enough to read this story for ourselves we've already rejected its message. This is almost certainly why the idea is presented in story form; otherwise we'd have no chance of recognizing and responding to its truth. It must be encountered in the form of a literary parable to bypass our self-protective (and self-destructive) faculties. Here, as in the parables of Jesus, much of the meaning of this story is hidden—and hidden on purpose—so that only those with ears to hear will discover the treasure within.

The Central Conflict of Scripture

The central conflict of the entire biblical story is the fate of God's creation—*all* his creation. That which he created as "good" (or *tov*: beautiful, good, and true) would be ruled over and cared for by those he created in his image as "very good"—in other words, by humans.

> Then God said, "Let us make mankind in our image, in our
> likeness, so that they may rule over the fish in the sea and the

birds in the sky, over the livestock and all the wild animals, and over all the creatures that move along the ground." (Gen. 1:26)

Adam and Eve have been given authority to rule as representatives of God's divine authority. They are king and queen of the whole world, and the world itself is a place of duality, with Eden as the pivot point or connecting middle where heaven and earth overlap.

In the very center of this middle place of overlapping contexts—the place where heaven kisses earth—God plants two trees that are saturated in literary significance.

> And the LORD God made all kinds of trees grow out of the ground—trees that were pleasing to the eye and good for food. In the middle of the garden were the tree of life and the tree of the knowledge of good and evil. (Gen. 2:9)

Here we have not only two trees but two very different ways of understanding what these trees represent. The tree of life is perhaps not difficult to wrap one's mind around; later we'll learn that to eat from that tree is to "live forever" (Gen. 3:22).

But the tree of the knowledge of good and evil is more difficult, in part because the combination of words that describe it—knowledge, good, evil—are themselves easily perceived as distinct and separate ideals, two of which are universal goods. We assume, quite unconsciously, that both *knowledge* and *good* should be placed on the positive side of the moral compass.

This raises a biting question: Why has God declared off-limits the knowledge of not just evil but also good? Doesn't he want moral creatures ruling in his stead?

But we must remember that there are two trees, and those trees stand in contradistinction. It is only the tree of the knowledge of good and evil that has been forbidden. Adam and Eve are free to eat from the tree of life, but they choose not to.

And the LORD God commanded the man, "You are free to eat from any tree in the garden; but you must not eat from the tree of the knowledge of good and evil, for when you eat of it you will certainly die." (Gen. 2:16–17)

All this is a setup for the conflict that will follow, first through Eve's dilemma, then through the consequences of Adam and Eve's submission to the serpent's deception. It's worth mentioning that Eve's decision isn't a true dramatic dilemma in the sense of being a choice between two terrible alternatives. Instead, it's a tragic dilemma, for it demonstrates the tragedy of an avoidable catastrophe caused by a wrong moral choice.

An astute observer will notice that Eve and then Adam both make a decision requiring some knowledge of moral imperatives. If they didn't yet know right from wrong, their decision to eat from that tree could not itself be wrong. The traditional answer to this question is that they had the command of God not to eat from it, therefore they didn't need to know right and wrong for themselves. They knew enough to rely on the good and wise counsel of God himself. This in turn implies that the tree represents something quite different from what we expected at first. Indeed, a superficial reading of the story is likely to create confusion about what's really happening, which is why the story must be read as a story.

Lust to the Eyes

The answer to what the tree really offers is, ironically, found in the temptation spoken to Eve by the serpent. Robert Alter's translation of Genesis 3:4–7 reads:

"You shall not be doomed to die. For God knows that on the day you eat of it your eyes will be opened and you will become as gods knowing good and evil." And the woman saw that the

tree was good for eating and that it was lust to the eyes, and the
tree was lovely to look at, and she took of the fruit and ate, and
she also gave to her man, and he ate. And the eyes of the two
were opened, and they knew they were naked, and they sewed
fig leaves and made themselves loincloths.[1]

The serpent's promise in verse 5 was that they would "become as gods knowing good and evil." Other translations often
render this "you will be like God, knowing good and evil." The
difference lies in the ambiguity of the underlying word *elohim*,
which can mean either "God" or "gods." If read as "God," the
temptation is an accusation that God is trying to prevent the
humans from being like him, which is something of an absurdity
given that they were already created in his image. (Then again,
temptation is often absurd, especially in hindsight.) But if it is
read as "gods," then the temptation is more of an invitation, for
the serpent is presenting an offer of solidarity for the humans
to join an ongoing rebellion. We will discover in chapter 6 that
heaven may have already experienced a division within its "divine
council"[2] as certain "sons of God"[3]—themselves spirit beings—
have turned away from the Creator. *Join us*, the serpent seems
to be saying, *in our fight to define good and evil for ourselves!*

Either way, this latter statement is the point, for the tree of
knowing good and evil is not a shortcut to such knowledge
but a detour around it. The tree they have been told not to eat
from is too often misunderstood as an endowment of moral
wisdom. It isn't. What the tree represents is the act of throwing
off God's definitions of good and evil in order to make those
distinctions independently. It is the tree of deciding for yourself
what you will call good and evil.

This is why the tree appears so beautiful, its fruit so delicious.
This is why it is "lust to the eyes." More importantly, this is the
key to understanding the explosion of evil that overtakes the
world immediately after they eat from it.

Most of our moral problems are rooted in our human, perhaps innate, desire to place the moral compass of the universe
within ourselves. Our stories get off track when they seduce
us into viewing everything through the lens of a protagonist's
desires and well-being. But such stories are still attractive; it
isn't difficult to convince us that what's good for Paula Protagonist must be good and right. After all, we already believe
that what's good for ourselves must be morally right, and what
is a protagonist if not a projection of the self?

The story of Eden is the setup for human history because it
points to the underlying root of our collective problem: each of us
believes that we're qualified to be the moral center of the universe.

But however brilliant or wise or virtuous you are, you can
never know all the factors that go into what makes something
good or evil. We see in part and we experience in part. Our
perspective as humans is always limited. We think we see the
whole moral equation, but something has always been left out.

This is why the very claim to "know good and evil" is itself
evil. It's why Google's original motto, "Don't be evil," was a
trap. It is *always* a trap, because when you're the arbiter of right
and wrong, you'll always find ways to define evil as the things
you're not doing or the things your enemy is doing.

Throughout the Old Testament, God implores his people to
do "what is right in my eyes" (1 Kings 11:33). When they do
what is right in their own eyes, the results are catastrophic, as
the book of Judges attests.

If this surrender to moral relativism were the only thing happening between the serpent and the humans, the story would
be dire enough. But the situation is actually much worse.

Joining the Demonic Rebellion

Our Enlightenment rationalism and materialist philosophy have
mythologized the spiritual dimension that's taken for granted in

this story. Without a demonic realm and a conflict larger than the disobedience of God's naive children, the story doesn't hold together. It's true that eating from the wrong tree has devastating consequences, but those consequences weren't limited to generational "fallenness." The story of the fall isn't merely that humanity broke its own innocence. The story of the fall is the story of how the first human regents surrendered their dominion authority to a demonic rebellion hell-bent on misusing it.

Adam and Eve were given divine rulership on earth. In yielding to the serpent's deception, they handed that authority to God's spiritual adversaries. We know very little from the Bible about what these adversaries look like or what this resistance to God's plan entailed. Paul refers to them as "rulers" and "powers" and "spiritual forces of evil in the heavenly realms" (Eph. 6:12). We also know that in the New Testament Jesus calls Satan the "evil one" (Matt. 13:19) and "the prince of this world" (John 12:31), and implies that Satan has at his disposal a hierarchy of powerful and wicked spirit agents (Mark 3:23, 26). But we aren't given significant glimpses behind the spiritual curtain, and we must accept this fact as intentional; what we aren't told is also part of the unfolding story.

What we *are* told is that after eating the forbidden fruit the first humans were cut off from the tree of life by "cherubim and a flaming sword flashing back and forth" (Gen. 3:24).

So God has placed two trees in the middle of the garden of Eden, the place where heaven and earth meet.

One is the tree of life. The first humans don't eat from the tree of life when they can, and later the way to it is barred. Though they're never commanded *not* to eat from the tree of life, the path to that tree is cut off.

The other tree is the tree of the knowledge of good and evil, and they're warned not to eat from it lest they die. The serpent promises they won't die but will instead become like the gods, knowing good and evil.

Notice that the tree of the knowledge of good and evil is connected to a perceived *power*, something that equates to godhood, as well as to death. The tree of life is connected only to life; no other power is implied.

Madeleine L'Engle's description of the two kinds of power may prove helpful here:

> In so-called primitive societies there are two words for power, *mana* and *taboo*: the power which creates and the power which destroys; the power which is benign and the power which is malign. Odd that we have retained in our vocabulary the word for dangerous power, taboo, and have lost mana. Power always has both of these aspects, as the storyteller knows. . . . It is this double aspect of power which the artist must be brave enough to explore.[4]

If L'Engle is right, then *mana* and *taboo* are really just different words for *cosmos* and *chaos*, for what I will call *ideals* or *values* or *principles* on the one hand and *unprincipled power* on the other. Thus we might diagram the thematic nature of these trees as embodiments of an unexpected revelation.

Two things make this diagram surprising. First, naked power is aligned with the serpent, not with the Creator. I say this is surprising because we tend to assume that all power resides in the hands of God. But if power here is the sort that's uncontrolled and chaotic, then it cannot be a characteristic of the Lord God.

The Tree of Life		The Tree of the Knowledge of Good & Evil
LIFE		DEATH
Principle		Power
Cosmos		Chaos
Mana		Taboo

Second, it appears that both good and evil stand opposed to life. But it isn't really these traits that oppose life; it is the *knowledge* of good and evil arrived at through one's own wisdom or personal preference.

The Tree of Power Versus Power

Story uses multiple structural layers to communicate meaning. It aims to affect the mind through the heart, which means it's always working in parallel worlds, both through direct access (the "low road" of emotion) and through indirect access (the "high road" of reason).[5] If these seem backward, it's probably because we've been taught to distrust our emotions and depend only on our faculties of reason for objective truth.

Thematically, I would suggest there's a deeper level of storytelling that derives from the conflicting nature of our broken humanity. Humanity has developed two contrasting formulas for the exploration of reality through a story's theme. These formulas operate in the background, their influence so pervasive and so subtle that audiences are effectively blind to them.

The first formula is the dominant one found in most superhero movies and commercial fiction. It pits a hero, the embodiment of principled power, against some villain who is endowed with unprincipled power. The Avengers, for instance, must overcome Thanos to restore order to the world. Captain America must take down Red Skull. Spiderman must defeat Green Goblin.

This sort of simple storytelling doesn't imply the lack of a clear theme. On the contrary, deep thematic resonance can be conveyed even through still images.

Take, for example, the prerelease movie poster for *Man of Steel*, which depicts a handcuffed Superman standing between heavily armed soldiers. Over his right shoulder a brilliant flare of light illuminates his face even as it shadows those of his apparent captors. He could break the cuffs without effort, without really trying. Perhaps he's trying *not* to break them. And why? Because their restraint is symbolic, not literal, and the meaning of that symbolism is both obvious and subtle. Obvious because the tension is so intentional. We're *meant* to wonder what it means that Superman is handcuffed. How has he run afoul of the law? And to what sort of law can he be held accountable? If he has done something immoral, he is no longer Superman but a villain. Since this is unimaginable, we're left to ponder a more startling and disruptive question, namely, What if the law to which Superman must answer is itself corrupt? Can he be the Superman we've come to know and respect if he stands in opposition to human authority? But in that case, what do we have to rely on?

There is only one Superman, but the wheels of government, of the justice system, of our whole order of civilization, must go on grinding or there will be nothing left for those of us who are not superhuman. Even a bad government (and all governments are bad in their own way, though some are much worse than others) is better than anarchy. That at least is one of the basic assumptions of every culture. Things could be worse, and "worse" will arrive quickly in the absence of a restraining system.

So this poster of Superman in handcuffs overflows with dramatic tension in the form of implied questions and a visual dilemma. What will Superman do? And when he does it, what will we do in response? Whose side will we be on? And how can there even be a right answer to that question?

This at any rate is what the poster promises. In one image it implies a powerful underlying theme that fits a character like Superman, who is simultaneously archetypal and superhuman. And the theme it promises is that *Man of Steel* will be a story about principle versus power.

Sadly, the film is *not* a story about principle versus power. It is a story about principled power versus unprincipled power.

What begins in its first act as an examination of the right use of power (and of the dangerous effects power has on the human soul) has by its climax become an examination of how much collateral damage two superhumans would cause when beating each other senseless in a modern metropolis. In the beginning we're told that power is wondrous but also addictive and dangerous. By the end we're led to believe that what really matters is that the principled power must defeat the unprincipled power at any cost. Superman *must* win no matter how many people are crushed beneath the rubble of collapsed buildings in the process. And it is of course Superman who emerges victorious from the film's concluding CGI spectacle.

This thematic structure is not unique to superhero films. How many westerns end with some variation of a gunfight between a white hat and a black vest? How many war movies turn on some act of valor in which the protagonist single-handedly wipes out an enemy platoon? Courtroom dramas follow this pattern too, as do sports stories, heist stories, revenge stories, and even love stories.

What gives these narratives their power is a clear embodiment of good and evil that affirms the audience's natural inclination to place the center of the moral compass in the self. It's a seductive storytelling formula because it has the appearance of being right. Good versus evil is natural to us. At a glance we can see that such stories are "good for eating" and "lovely to look at." They are, to borrow Robert Alter's language, lust to the eyes. So we take the fruit and eat it, and when the good guy wins we cheer, regardless of the body count. It doesn't matter that in a story such as, say, *The Hunger Games*, those bodies belong to children who have been harvested by a corrupt government for the entertainment of the masses. They were on the wrong side. They were evil. And are we not entertained?

This is why I connect the first story formula to the tree of the knowledge of good and evil. I believe it derives directly from our addiction to deciding morality for ourselves. But it not only derives from that addiction, it encourages it.

The Tree of Power Versus Principle

The second formula is far less common in modern stories, and you can probably guess why. How does one create a story based on the tree of life?

The simple answer is found in the thematic structure of the story of the garden of Eden. Rather than pitting principled power against unprincipled power, tree of life stories set naked principle against naked power. Or, put another way, they set cosmos against chaos, mana against taboo.

In the classic movie *Mr. Smith Goes to Washington*, for example, we're presented with a protagonist who is stripped of reputation and community by the cruel machinations of a corrupt government and a colluding press, leaving Jimmy Stewart's boyish character nothing but his determination to tell the truth before a hostile Congress. Or take *Braveheart*, which begins with William Wallace hacking his way through perpetually evil English armies to defend his beloved Scotland, but ends by placing the will to be free, regardless of circumstances, as the moral center of its arc. And anyone who has read *The Lord of the Rings* (or watched the Peter Jackson adaptations) will understand that its central characters are not its powerful warriors and sorcerers but the simplehearted hobbits who refuse to give in to temptation.

Each of these is what I would call a tree of life story because its resolution depends on some pure principle or ideal—stripped of all external power—overcoming the sorts of power that seem to rule the world (e.g., money, influence, brawn).

Perhaps not surprisingly, I only began to notice the underlying difference between these two types of stories as a result of studying both Genesis and the works of four Christian novelists whose work heavily influenced the genres of fantasy and science fiction. These genres are my imaginative playground as a novelist, yet it still took me decades of study to recognize the common thread that ties George MacDonald to G. K. Chesterton, C. S. Lewis, and J. R. R. Tolkien. The latter two were friends at Oxford and critiqued each other's works regularly. And George MacDonald was so influential on literature that it should be no surprise many Christian writers in the early to middle twentieth century were impacted by his work.

But I'm not referring to whatever doctrinal or theological beliefs they held in common. I mean only that all four of these writers held to the tree of life formula described above. Chesterton, for example, is perhaps best known for his Father Brown mysteries, which have a priest as their sleuth protagonist. Father Brown uses his knowledge of humanity to solve crimes. But Brown's objective is never merely the solving of the crime. It is restoration. In "The Hammer of God," Brown solves the crime and then leaves justice to the perpetrator, not to the police. He's more concerned with the man's standing before God than before a human court. Or take *Manalive*, Chesterton's novel of a supposed criminal who turns out to have broken only the laws of humankind, not the laws of heaven.

I could list many examples, but perhaps one more will make the point better than a longer list, for this particular story is well-known and has been told both as a tree of life story and as a tree of knowledge story.

The Lion, the Witch, and the Wardrobe was the first book C. S. Lewis wrote in the Chronicles of Narnia series. In it four children go through the back of a wardrobe into a fantasy world ruled by a terrible villain, the White Witch, who has put a spell over the land to make it always winter and never Christmas. What makes the book a fascinating study in formula is that on close inspection it turns out to be a tree of life story. That is, the book draws all its power from the relationship between the children and Aslan. Their journey is a discovery of both the Great Lion and of themselves in relation to him. The real conflict in the book—all its dramatic tension—derives from the fact that Aslan seems to have disappeared from Narnia. And yet there are whispers: *Aslan is on the move!* The talking animals and other fairy creatures whisper in secret that he is coming, and coming soon. But will it be soon enough?

Indeed, it is sooner than we expect, for Aslan arrives in time to make a deal with the Witch to rescue the traitorous boy Edmund, life for life. And the point is not that this is an allegory for Christ (though it obviously is), but that the conflict isn't one of power defeating power. It's one of principle defeating power.

In the 2005 movie version of the story, the filmmakers missed this. Instead of Aslan arriving to set things right in Narnia, Aslan arrives to defeat the Witch. This may seem a small point, but it really is gigantic. The film makes evil the problem and goodness the solution. It places the climax of the conflict at the moment when Aslan devours (off-screen) the White Witch. As an affirmation that good is better than evil, this change works. And perhaps it was a natural change to make when adapting the more internal journey of a novel into the more external images of a film. Still, the effect is profound in the way it deals with the original theme of the story. Instead of the children going to Narnia to encounter Aslan, they have gone to Narnia to help win a war. They are no longer types of "true humans"—"sons of Adam" and "daughters of Eve"—as we were all meant to be.[6] They are instead children of royal birthright who embody the ideals of the tree of the knowledge of good and evil. Meanwhile, the invitation to life through relationship with Aslan has been removed from the story.

Perhaps this shouldn't be surprising. We are no longer in the garden of Eden, after all. And which of us can claim that we haven't eaten from the wrong tree ourselves? Or that our predisposition to judging our neighbor is the fault of our ancestors?

Sons of Adam and daughters of Eve indeed!

If we are to be pitied, it isn't because we had no choice in siding with the satanic rebellion after the first humans surrendered their authority to the Evil One. On the contrary, we're pitiable because we've deceived ourselves with a lie that's so easily refuted.

CONTEXT

5

THE ROAD TO RELEVANCE

As a lifelong student of the English language, I'm afflicted with an incurable admiration for Shakespeare. Though it isn't his best play in technical terms, *Macbeth* is my favorite, perhaps because back in the eighth grade, that was the play that convinced me literature could be cool. Here were witches and battles and murderous madness and prophetic omens and all manner of deception. Even though it was wrapped in antiquated language and phrases that escaped my comprehension entirely, I still loved the sometimes simple artistry of the Bard's turns of phrase and the dramatic tension that kept me striving to unlock what he was actually saying. Why was this story—with blood that would not come off the queen's hands and demonic tormentors and a protagonist who embraced evil in spite of the fact he knew it to be wrong—considered a great work of art?

The answer I would give now differs greatly from the one I would've given back then, which probably had more to do with the witches and the sword fighting than with anything related to the play's theme.

My reason for loving *Macbeth* now is due in large part to its frank depiction of the nihilism that results from an abandonment of ultimate meaning. Nowhere is that depiction clearer than when Macbeth learns that his wife the queen is dead and laments the news as coming at a bad time. And what has all his striving and "vaulting ambition" led him to? Has success without purpose, without a morality pinned to absolute standards, produced any happiness in his life? On the contrary.

> Tomorrow, and tomorrow, and tomorrow
> Creeps in this petty pace from day to day
> To the last syllable of recorded time,
> And all our yesterdays have lighted fools
> The way to dusty death. Out, out, brief candle!
> Life's but a walking shadow, a poor player
> That struts and frets his hour upon the stage
> And then is heard no more. It is a tale
> Told by an idiot, full of sound and fury,
> Signifying nothing.[1]

Macbeth might be speaking here for all of Western culture. Meaning is currently being sucked out of our lives, and at an alarming rate. Still more alarming is the fact that few people seem to understand why or how. We see the sickness but cannot name the disease.

Why this is happening may be open to debate. But *how* it is happening—the cause of all this sucking—is not mysterious at all. We're telling the wrong stories. We're erasing the lines that connect the imaginary to the real. We have replaced ultimate meaning with personal preference. We have, in other words, divorced relevance from context.

Our stories are technically excellent but thematically empty. They are no longer vehicles for reflecting the hard and beautiful truths of reality. Instead, they are stimulants, distracting daydreams, the siren songs of what we want to hear.

Our stories are a kind of dramatic witchcraft that offers kingship through dishonest flattery. As Banquo, Macbeth's lieutenant, puts it, "And oftentimes, to win us to our harm, the instruments of darkness tell us truths, win us with honest trifles, to betray [us] in deepest consequence."[2] We see the maddening effects of that betrayal everywhere as the context of reality begins to collapse under the weight of all the fantasies imposed upon it.

It's by the pricking of our own thumbs that something wicked this way comes.

Making Reality Irrelevant

We're shaped by stories, and we use stories to shape our understanding of reality. We *build* meaning in layers, and we *interpret* meaning in layers. This is why, if you have to go to the restroom in the middle of a movie, when you return you always ask, "What did I miss?" You need those basic layers to correctly interpret what you see and hear later.

The reason you need those basic layers is that *everything in a story is meaningful*. Playwright Anton Chekhov memorably expressed this dramatic principle—now known as Chekhov's gun—when he said, "If in the first act you have hung a pistol on the wall, then in the following one it should be fired. Otherwise don't put it there."[3]

This is part of the attraction of immersive storytelling. Anyone who has felt transported to another world while reading will readily understand the pull of Middle-earth or Narnia or Hogwarts. The narrative wizardry that brings such worlds to life isn't merely that in the imagination all the senses may be fired, but that such firings are, in those other worlds, always meaningful, always significant, always pointing outside themselves to something important.

This sort of all-encompassing significance is what we long for. We want life to be meaningful. And it seems that for much of human history it was. For a time, anyway, people lived as if happenstance didn't happen, but only the ordered story arcs of a trillion trillion atoms in relation to a divine order. In his book *Saving the Appearances*, philosopher and Inkling Owen Barfield writes,

> Before the scientific revolution, the world was more like a garment men wore about them than a stage on which they moved. . . . Compared with us, they felt themselves and the objects around them and the words that expressed those objects, immersed together in something like a clear lake of—what shall we say?—of "meaning" if you choose.[4]

This attraction to meaning, even where it may not really exist or where we may not fully recognize it, is what makes stories not just powerful but addictive.

Life is far more complicated than any story. In a sense, it is *too* complicated to function with the simplicity of a story. Which is to say that if everything in life is meaningful, it wouldn't be possible to recognize all the meanings happening around us at any given moment. Thus it may be the preponderance of meaning in reality that shatters our perception of life as an unfolding story. There is simply too much all at once.

But the more important point is that to the postmodern reader Barfield's "clear lake of meaning" is absurd. We don't see reality as a garment to be worn, a natural shell for a supernatural identity. Our lake of reality isn't clear. Perhaps it's not even a lake but more like a polluted soup of contradictions. We don't subscribe practically to the blind determinism of naturalism, which would destroy our sense of autonomy and self-direction, but neither are we willing to accept the rigid orthodoxies that shaped the world of the Middle Ages. Postmodernists would rather be hopeless than gullible.

Still, one must have something to live for, some reason for crawling out of bed in the morning. For many, purpose is packaged in the next generation or in the emotional pay-off of meeting a private moral standard—raising one's children, say, or volunteering for a nonprofit. But what standard makes these ultimately meaningful? Which compass of ideals is shaping the story goal of my life? Is it the mere *decision* to see family and good works as meaningful, or is there some yardstick beyond my desires and emotions and beliefs that makes them so?

But even supposing we accept the existential answer that life is what we make of it, how many children or soup kitchens does it take to create a worthwhile life, and how often do these end goals appear in the drama of day-to-day living? How much of one's life is spent impacting the next generation or lending a helping hand? Isn't life mostly filled with missed appointments that turn out not to have been very important after all, and with food that's neither good nor bad, and with loaded pistols that never go off?

The insurance adjuster who sinks into her cubicle for a dreary shift handling medical claims may do so out of commitment to spouse and children. Perhaps here and there the odd file may stand out as a case for extra attention or even as a job well done. But the steady grind of bureaucratic tedium, the weight of artificially imposed goals, the relentless avalanche of interoffice emails and team meetings and project updates—all these begin to look like nothing more than random molecules in a cloud of dust. Is the stapler meaningful? The office party? The coffee-stained desk that has lasted longer than any single employee?

You can bet a story protagonist wouldn't have to deal with the stapler unless he were dusting it for fingerprints, and if he attended the office party it would only be to meet the love of his life.

In short, it has become increasingly difficult to see the point of *anything* unless it is packaged as a first-person shooter or a seven-season TV series.

Our response to this evaporation of meaning has been disastrous. Rather than reexamining our presuppositions about life or even looking for significance in unexpected places, we have shifted our search to a different, more arbitrary realm. Instead of using stories as tools for the discovery of ultimate meaning in reality, we are using reality as a tool for the invention of subjective meanings in stories.

We're making reality irrelevant.

Overlapping Contexts

Technically, a story's context is everything that happens before and after the current moment. This means context not only encompasses the other four story elements as they exist prior to the *now*, but also that audiences understand it, for the most part, only as background information. Even English teachers tend to consider the context of a story either in terms of its setting (i.e., its internal location, time period, culture, situation) or through some historical or critical microscope (e.g., How might a Marxist view of economics shape our reading of *The Merchant of Venice?*).

Setting is of course vital to storytelling because an audience must know certain details in order to imaginatively participate in the cocreation of a story. In fact, one hallmark of beginning writers is the failure to create minimal setting details, which is why first novels often suffer from white-fog backdrops, inconsistent time-stamping, and cultural stereotypes. These shatter a story's illusion of reality.

But what concerns us here is the nature of context as layered meaning and how that impacts our interpretation of a story. Context isn't just the corkboard detritus of everything found in, say, a writer's My Novel folder. Context is the deliberate and orderly creation of stacked meaning that results from characters and images and events being arranged in a particular chronological order.

When a story's internal context (i.e., the fictional reality within the story world) intersects with the external context of real life, the reader experiences relevance. Those places a story has resonated with you as true or as directly meaningful in your own life almost certainly happened because of this overlap.

Because every reader brings a different set of life experiences to a story, those moments of relevance vary from person to person. This doesn't mean such moments are unpredictable. Writers and other storytellers *intend* for their work to be relevant. They know what causes emotion. In fact, you can actually see where these intentional moments of relevance hit audiences if you know where to look.

For instance, I read John Green's novel *The Fault in Our Stars* just a few weeks after it was published. I read it on my Kindle with the public highlights feature turned on. The last page of the story showed me clear evidence that relevance can be designed: one particular sentence had been highlighted almost 19,000 times. And those were just the people who took the trouble to highlight those words and had made their highlights publicly visible. That's relevance in action. It's the story reaching outside itself to create meaning in the lives of an audience.

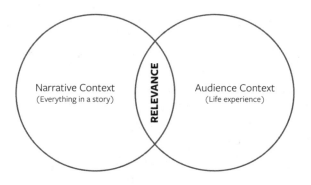

But we are no longer striving for this sort of overlap except in our propaganda. Instead, contemporary storytelling seems to be rapidly, and perhaps intentionally, moving toward a complete separation of contextual domains. In other words, our experience of meaning may soon be largely disconnected from anything real.

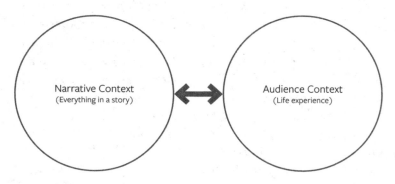

This isn't difficult to imagine. All that's required is for every story to stop portraying shared *classes* of experience and begin to create private, *customized* experiences based on emotional and sensory stimulation. We are already seeing this, I would argue, in the cinematic depiction of spectacle over story that characterizes many blockbuster movies.

The architects of this brave new story world have created pipelines for an endless supply of content in which everything is superficially meaningful. We're being given technically refined stories in which every stapler and office party is *subjectively* meaningful—because everything inside those stories is tightly controlled.

The Road to Relevance

This, I think, is how meaning is being stripped from our culture: by a series of storytelling shifts that move the context of our stories further and further from the internal/external self (mind/body) to the external projection of self—to avatars of individual identity.

The first step was to remove our stories from the realm of the imagination to the realm of the senses. When reading a novel, for instance, we must engage the mind's eye and experience the descriptions, dialogue, and exposition internally or we will abandon the story altogether. One must imagine the goblins and forests and battles of Middle-earth to experience *The Lord of the Rings* as it was written. But if you're watching the film version, very little is required except that you keep your eyes open. All the imagining has already been done by the producers and actors and digital artists before the movie even starts. This is why I call it a first step. A story experienced on a silver screen has been removed from the internal world of the imagination to the external world of the audiovisual.

We are long past this first step. A cinema is a physical space that carries its own sensory thumbprint: the smell of popcorn, the sticky residue of fountain drinks underfoot, the dramatic lighting of curtains and aisles. A movie theater is at least a real building situated in a geographic space. Today we carry cinemas in our pockets. Which means we can experience a spectacle story almost anywhere, at any time—on an airplane or in bed or sitting across from one's spouse at a restaurant. We no longer need a specific context, a socially acceptable time and place that's appropriate for consuming a story, because stories are now available in *every* time and place. We carry an endless supply of them in our digital devices.

But we are further along than even this. It isn't just that our stories have been moved outward to our senses, or even that our consumption of stories is no longer connected to physical times and places. The third step has been the removal of the audience itself to a virtual realm. In fact, we're seeing the early migration of human identities from physical bodies to digital

97

avatars. The body and soul are being rended not through death but through a displacement of identity.

Millennials were the first to experience this third step. Gen Z is further along still, having started the process at an earlier age and in a more effective form. It isn't just that children are being raised on screens or that they consume stories in the form of video games and apps and streaming programs. The larger problem is that their entire lives are increasingly experiences online. Education, socialization, entertainment, activism, relational intimacy—all these are being off-loaded to virtual space. The tablet isn't just a device; it's a window into an alternate reality where anyone's identity can be tailor-made. Consequently, the context of many people's real lives, especially that of many teens, is digital experiences projected outside the skin.

In his book *Hollowed Out*, educator Jeremy Adams writes of today's young people, "They live largely solitary lives, inextricably connected to their phones but largely disconnected from parents, churches, and communities. Instead, they eat alone, they study alone, they even socialize alone in a virtual world untethered to the physical."[5] While this characterization may be hyperbolic, it nonetheless reveals why it's helpful to understand the importance of overlapping contexts. For those who are off-loading their embodied experiences to the internet, a story will feel artificially meaningful when that internal context (what happens in a video game) overlaps with their experiences in other virtual spaces. Relevance isn't perceived as a connection between a story and your real, embodied life, but between a story and everything you've experienced online. As long as Kate identifies sufficiently as KittnLover232, and as long as the events and people of a virtual story world point outside that world to other experiences in her virtual space, she will feel a temporary sense of relevance suggestive of absolute meaning. That sense is an illusion for the simple reason that KittnLover232 is not Kate, however much of herself she plugs into it.

Still, an artificial sense of meaning may seem better than no meaning at all, especially in a world where the collective library of stories is almost limitless. The downside of a lifetime spent scratching this existential itch is that you can never be sufficiently provoked to uncover the source of the rash. Artificial purpose may feel good, but it isn't good if it keeps you from finding the real thing. This is why I say that these new story strategies are doomed to fail. They may be effective at satisfying the lust for spectacle and raw sensation that drives our baser instincts—what Elon Musk calls the monkey brain—but they cannot make the leap from virtual to physical. Kate may spend a great deal of her time as KittnLover232, but the reverse is impossible. KittnLover232 will never attempt to be Kate. In short, you cannot get full by watching a projection of yourself eat, no matter how delicious the food appears to be.

Stories are buckets for meaning. They're designed to overlap with the real world. This is why our stories today are failing so badly to satisfy our need for meaning and purpose. Our stories are rich only in subjective meaning, not ultimate meaning, because subjective meaning is the only kind our storytellers can imagine. Consequently, our thirst for something transcendent isn't quenched. The two sorts of meaning, subjective and ultimate, are simply not interchangeable. They're as different as salt water and fresh. Indeed, the time is perhaps not far off when we will have "Water, water, every where, / Nor any drop to drink."[6]

There is only one way to end this consuming thirst and starvation diet, at least in story terms, and that is to begin at once drinking fresh water and eating real, nourishing food, not just the junk food offerings of our cultural vending machines. We must insist that reality is not just *a* domain but *the* domain, the *natural* domain of story. Madeleine L'Engle asserts, "All of life is story, story unraveling and revealing meaning."[7] We must demand true relevance.

This means acknowledging what the language of story has been telling us all along. The sort of meaning we long for— especially in the here and now of our confusion and pain and boredom—is not unattainable or illusory. Reality is more than a random explosion of matter or blind determinate chemistry.

Story is telling us this. That is one of its functions, to remind us that the road to relevance is overlapping contexts. And not just human contexts or even the metacontexts of digital spaces and massive catalogs of streaming entertainment. True relevance is only possible in a real world beyond our control and thus part of a story so large it can only be understood by those who dare to live within it.

Parallel Truth

We're born into a universe of parallel realities, of overlapping contexts that sometimes express themselves openly and other times only shimmer like heat rising from a distant tarmac. However we conceive of heaven and earth, spirit and flesh, or the alternate dimensions of speculative fiction, the language of story seems to depend on such pairings for its existence as an art form.

Parallel worlds are the stuff of art because they communicate the reality of life. This is one reason stories are effective when they speak honestly about humanity, regardless of our worldview or faith. The world is gritty and cruel, yet innocence and goodness may be found within it.

This is the paradox of art; it is the central technique of truth-telling from which every application of parallelism draws its power. To reveal something true about life, the artist presents an alternate vision that somehow communicates the coexistence of distinct and opposing realities.

Irony, for instance, is the loading of a situation or symbol or event with opposite meanings, so that we are simultaneously inspired in conflicting but compatible emotions. For example, a bittersweet ending is ironic because it resolves in a way that is both happy and sad. Is it possible to be happy and sad in the same moment? Yes, of course. Otherwise we would not be able to feel the power of the bittersweet ending. More importantly, bittersweet is a snapshot of life. Reality is a mixture, and that mixture is felt most powerfully in the paradoxical convergence of its extremes.

Or take juxtaposition, the technique of setting two unrelated things side by side in order to imply a connection. Advertisers often use juxtaposition to make claims that would be illegal if stated as a fact: This beer makes you young and fit. These cookies will help you lose weight. This streaming service will ensure you find the ideal spouse.

At the heart of every great truth stands a paradox. In my classes with Leonard Sweet, I've heard him go so far as to say that "orthodoxy is paradoxy." But often these paradoxes are hidden in ways that require the insight and metaphorical vision of the artist to reveal. Psychiatrist Iain McGilchrist suggests that these paradoxes are hardwired into the parallel left-right hemispheres of our brains:

> There are needs, drives, or tendencies, which, while equally fundamental, are also fundamentally incompatible: an essentially divisive drive to acquisition, power and manipulation, based on competition, which sets individual against individual, in the service of unitary survival; and an essentially cohesive drive towards co-operation, synergy and mutual benefit, based on collaboration, in the service of the survival of the group. . . . Both of these drives or tendencies can serve us well, and each expresses an aspect of the human condition that goes right to the core.[8]

Gerard Manley Hopkins said that "the artificial part of poetry, perhaps we shall be right to say all artifice, reduces itself to the principle of parallelism."[9] Every great storyteller seems to wrestle with this quirk of reality. I would go so far as to say that it is only in the aftermath of this wrestling that one's artistic voice achieves maturity. Before their songs or paintings or movies or novels will resonate deeply with an audience, the musician or painter or writer must grapple with the angel of the Lord and not let go, must have their hip wrenched and their name changed from "Jacob the Deceiver" to "Israel the One Who Contends with God."

This is the price of truth-telling: the storyteller must not place their thumb on the scale. They must not take sides against the darkness and the chaos nor against the light and the cosmos, but must speak or sing or write or paint fairly that which is real and true. The only way to do this is to paint in complementary colors; to perform in twin clefs the harmony as well as the melody; to write of the beauty of the world but also of its ugliness.

Parallel Opposition

Because reality is bidimensional, truth can only really be told in parallel. Matter and spirit mirror body and soul as Christ and the church mirror heaven and earth. In their foreword to William Edgar's *A Supreme Love*, Carl and Karen Ellis riff on this idea when they write,

> We experience life in parallels: the formal and the dynamic, unity and diversity, form and freedom, the one and the many, and on and on. Great thinkers throughout history have wrestled with these parallels, asking, "Which one prevails in our reality?" From God's limitless perspective, two realities can fulfill, harmonize, and dance with each other because they are creations of the unlimited Being, namely, God himself.[10]

This is why the story that ends with a deus ex machina resolution treats its audience with contempt. Life isn't like this, or at least cannot be depended on to be like this. That people sometimes experience a happy ending is not in question. The question rather is this: What is the true nature of things, and how often do the gods emerge from a trapdoor to set things right just when things are at their worst? Perhaps it *has* happened, but it is not *what* happens.

Someone will say, "But consider Christ!" To which I reply that (1) Christ did not set things right by the mechanism of imposed justice or outside agency but by submission to all that the forces of antagonism threw at him, and (2) Christ is the Deus *in* machina. He is the God who *enters* the machine, not the god who emerges from it.

My graduate school mentor, James Gunn, used to say, "The hero must be the method of his own salvation." As a young Christian, this annoyed me. Did he not know that Christ is the only moderator capable of effecting our salvation? I knew of course that Gunn was using the word "salvation" in a story sense. He spoke of resolution, not redemption.

What most irritated me was that I knew he was right but could not at first formulate why nor understand how that idea might fit within a Christian worldview. Eventually I saw what should have been obvious all along: Fictional characters are not real people. Furthermore, protagonists are not even meant to *represent* real people. Instead, a protagonist's main function is to embody an ideal, to demonstrate the types of experiences we encounter in real life when principle and power collide.

This is why the hero must effect his own rescue at the climax. If truth cannot stand on its own two feet, then it is not worth pursuing. If forgiveness is really better than revenge, why should the protagonist who embodies it need to be rescued by a squad of Marines? Or again, if love is really stronger than hatred and selfishness, why must it depend upon someone else for its salvation?

No. It is only when truth prevails *in spite of* its earthly impotence that we see truth clearly revealed. When forgiveness has nothing going for it but its own nature—when nothing about forgiveness makes sense but the helpless victim of a story forgives her oppressor anyway—then we recognize the truth-in-parallel of an honest storyteller. When Love remains nailed to a cross and refuses the injunction to save himself, only then has the hero become the method of his own salvation—and perhaps that of the audience as well.

Great stories thus employ techniques of parallelism to express the parallel nature of truth in reality. But notice: what they align in parallel are actually opposites in spectrum. The things running side by side in a story (e.g., joy/sorrow, life/death, truth/falsehood, light/darkness) are polar opposites harmonized through tension. But instead of separating, they run together like railroad tracks.

Dorothy L. Sayers writes, "The vital power of an imaginative work demands a diversity within its unity; and the stronger the diversity, the more massive the unity."[11] Dramatically speaking, opposites attract. And it is the tension found in this simultaneous attraction and opposition that makes a story interesting, because we in the audience are always off-balance and internally looking for a sense of resolution between the two. Which will win out, the love between Romeo and Juliet or the hatred of their feuding families? Will Jekyll or Hyde prevail? Can humans control nature, or will the chaos inherent in reality spring a T-Rex from its Jurassic Park cage? Might life be beautiful even in death? Could cancer be an agent of healing? What if someone told you that an electric chair once set them free? How about a cross?

The interesting thing about each of these is that they seem to be models of *logos*,[12] of bringing the opposites together in a way that doesn't just harmonize them but produces parallel distinctions. In dying, Romeo and Juliet are at last joined together, and so are their families—thus striking parallel notes of joy and sorrow. Humans may indeed control genetics but not the genetic by-products of their creation; the majesty of Hammond's island theme park is transformed into a place where past and future are juxtaposed, where wonder and horror coexist.

It turns out that the world we live in is a *Jurassic Park* reality of parallel opposition. Is it any wonder these parallels are found all through human history, encoded into our best stories and artwork? Doesn't it make sense that they would also be embedded structurally into the Bible?[13]

I suspect the Story of Stories was designed to reveal this to us. Scripture whispers in the very structure of its narratives that we live in a place of twin realities—a place of matter and of spirit, of life and of death, of chaos and of cosmos.

In the next chapter we'll begin to see why.

6

BEHOLD A WONDERFUL HIPPO!

The book of Job is the story of humanity.

Theologically, it serves many functions, not the least of which is establishing the context of the biblical through line—the story arc that runs from Genesis to Revelation. It's also a straightforward tale of faithfulness and a profound exploration of suffering. Job asks deep questions that speak to the existence of ultimate meaning and is rightly considered "wisdom literature."[1]

If you look further, dig deeper, and dare to read the story as a story, you will see much more: not only does the tale offer a prophetic depiction of the Messiah, it also establishes the basis of his victory over satanic dominion. And it does so through a narrative template that includes the two primary conflicting story patterns of history: chaos and cosmos.

But at its heart, Job serves an even broader vision, for it asks a question that must ultimately be answered by each of us: Is God good if he isn't good to *me*?

Some will take exception to this question on the grounds that God is always good to everyone. But from a human perspective, this phrasing captures the dilemma of meaningless suffering and must be dealt with. Is God always good? If so, why the Holocaust? Why cancer? Why the million faces of human evil?

In facing this question head-on, the book of Job establishes the context not only for Scripture but for all reality. It is a cosmological book that seeks to answer the unanswerable. But before the book can be navigated as Scripture, it must be experienced as a story.

Here, as elsewhere, it isn't the head that leads the way but the tale. To understand Job, you must let it break your heart. If it doesn't break your heart, you're probably reading it as sacred or wise or important without letting it first sap you of any confidence in human answers. Job is of course sacred and wise and important, but it is these things only later, after it is the story of a right-side-up man in an upside-down world.

So pull up a chair and listen to how the story goes down . . .

Job's Origin Story

Once upon a time there was this really great guy named Job. When I say he was great, I don't mean he was the sort of guy who would buy you a beer or come over for Sunday football. I don't mean he was someone who could keep a secret or knew how to tell a joke or was always ready to loan you his cordless drill.

No, no. Job was morally good. Not goody-two-shoes good or someone who always gave at the office good, but someone who gave his shoes away when nobody was looking. The sort of person who fed homeless people every day and then went home and cried because he couldn't do more for them. He carried other people's troubles even when they were beyond his help. Job was Mother Teresa with a beard, except that Job lived in the ancient world, a world so comparatively brutal that his goodness was almost blinding in contrast.

And why was that world so brutal?

Well, that's part of the story. Looking back, you could say that the reason was a lack of civil government; there were few enforceable laws and fewer police to enforce them. But that doesn't come close to describing the problem. You could say that slavery and murder were so commonplace that people assumed these atrocities were part of a divine order. Which is also sort of true. People no doubt felt the brokenness of the world but could find no explanation for it except that the gods probably intended it to be that way. To some, life must have seemed like a cosmic sitcom, and mortal humans were just serving the entertainment appetites of distant and unknowable masters.

What people couldn't see was that the source of their torments originated with a cosmic split in the heavenly realm. It wasn't God doing all this damage but a spirit being named Satan who, back before this story takes place, had somehow usurped the divine authority granted to humans and was now ruling the earth as a kind of demigod regent.

This wasn't what God—the real God—intended. But something had happened when Satan took over, and now a spiritual war was splitting apart both heaven and earth, with God claiming to be the source of things like goodness and justice and truth, and Satan claiming that these things never really mattered because, in the end, power is what drives the universe.

So when God looked down and saw how Job was living his life, he was delighted. It's one thing to be good in heaven where the presence of God is always tangible. It's quite another to be good on earth where the presence of evil lurks around every corner. But here was Job, doing all this good stuff anyway, and under such harsh conditions. Job daily shook his fist at the satanic ethic of do as you please and lived as a moral rebel, doing right instead of serving himself.

What made this even more impressive was that Job had no idea about the cosmic conflict taking place backstage. Because he could see neither God nor Satan, Job had to choose how to live his life based on the clues of physical reality. All he had to go on were his reason and his senses and his conscience.

You know how hard that is even in the modern world with our hospitals and Amazon deliveries and food banks. Imagine what that must have been like back then. Even God was impressed. In fact, God blessed Job in everything he did, as if to say, "Keep going! Keep being good! You are a great example for everyone else who has given up on the ideals of justice and mercy and integrity." So every time Job gave away his shoes, he discovered he'd somehow gotten twelve more pairs of size 10W Rockport loafers by the time he returned home.

Satan took this divine endorsement of Job personally, and he personally came to God's royal court just as the "sons of God" were presenting themselves. The accusation Satan brought appeared to be leveled at Job but was really an assault on God's character. It seems the "accuser" wanted more than dominion; he wanted to tear down the very basis of God's claim to authority.

Parallel Narration

This is the context developed in the opening chapters of Job. It is essential to understand this in some depth—that is, as a *story*—because even though the meaning of Job is directly connected to its dramatic structure, that meaning won't be clear if you look past the actors and strain to see the lights and wires of the stage.

For modern readers this presents an interesting problem. We're so familiar with the devices of contemporary storytelling that we overlook ones that ancient audiences took for granted.

Job utilizes three narrative devices, each one a different form of parallelism, and these provide the structural backbone for everything in the story.

1. Earth is a reflection of heaven.

The first device is a motif of *reflectivity*. What happens in the physical realm is a reflection of something that has already happened in the spiritual realm. Thematically, this *event parallelism* assumes a contradictory worldview from that of ancient magical cultures, which tried to force reflections in the spiritual realm by manipulating aspects of the physical one.

In Job we see the opposite. Instead of people changing the world of the gods, the human world is moved and shaped by an unseen otherness that precedes our physical experiences. The spirit world is mirrored in the physical world. Or, to put it from the human point of view, what happens on earth has, in some fashion, already happened in heaven.[2]

What happens in the opening two chapters is reproduced as the story unfolds. God's experience is mirrored, in part, through Job's. This motif establishes what's happening in the heavenly realm as the source of what will follow on earth. But instead of portraying a "heaven wills it" dynamic, the story presents a spiritual realm already divided and in conflict.

That earth is a reflection of heaven is essential context for the unfolding of Job's dramatic arc.

2. The chiastic structure of Job both conceals and reveals its theme.

Chiasmus, a form of *structural parallelism* that makes almost everything reflective, is common in the Bible.[3] It's not just heaven and earth that are mirrored; the first and last things are also mirror images of each other; the second and second-to-last things are likewise reflected; and so on until the middle of the story, which is the dramatic high point. Sometimes in a chiastic structure the middle contains a direct repetition; other times it stands alone. A paired center pushes the core idea to the edges; an unmatched middle highlights the center, or what is sometimes called the "central pivot."[4]

Put more simply, chiastic stories are like hamburgers assembled in a specific order: bun—sauce—hamburger patty—sauce—bun. The center, the single hamburger patty, is the main thing. We call this sort of sandwich a "hamburger," not a "bunburger" or "sauceburger."

The hamburger patty in the book of Job is found not quite in the center, but in the chiastic center—that is, the center of the pairings—which is chapter 28, the "Ode to Wisdom."[5] Structurally, the book of Job can be outlined with a simple chiastic pattern:

A Backstory
  B Confrontation
    C Temptation
      D Interlude (Ode to Wisdom)
    C′ Temptation
  B′ Confrontation
A′ Resolution

Its structure is more complicated than this, but for now this outline is enough to make the point. In Job, the first thing is the last thing, the second thing is the second-to-last thing, and so on, with the main theme highlighted by its place in the center.

Chiastic stories are probably meant to draw their dramatic power from being read aloud rather than consumed by readers scanning the text silently.[6] As David Dorsey points out, "An ancient was compelled to use structural signals that would be perceptible to the listening audience. Signals were geared for the ear, not the eye."[7]

3. Job is designed to unfold in layers.

The third literary device used in Job is *layering*, or *parallelism of meaning*. During the time of Jesus, rabbis read the Scriptures in a series of four layers intended to unfold chronologically:

1. *Peshat*—the **literal** meaning.
2. *Remez*—the **typological** meaning.
3. *Derash*—the **metaphorical** meaning associated with the midrash.
4. *Sod*—the **revelational** meaning, perhaps available to a student only through a spiritual experience of connection to and with God.[8]

In a sense, these are like Russian nesting dolls. What you see at first is only one doll, not four. The first doll, being the largest, is a container that houses the other three. But you cannot see the smaller dolls until you take apart the larger ones.

In order to understand the book of Job, we must begin with a literal interpretation of its story, which means we must take seriously the context of its opening.

The Villain of Job

The first six verses of Job establish Job's righteousness, the scope of his great riches, and his concern for the spiritual well-being of his seven sons and three daughters, whom he suspects may be living unrighteously. This short introduction is the story's opening bookend. Dramatically, it functions as a prologue rather than a first chapter. It gives us context for the civil war that's about to erupt in heaven.

And we need that context to understand what happens next, when the narrative pulls back the curtain of God's divine chamber to reveal a three-way conflict between God, his "sons," and the Adversary, Satan. This contextual setup is undiluted drama. God's sons have come before him—"and Satan came also with them" (Job 1:6)!

When Darth Vader walks into the room, we know something bad is about to happen. When Shakespeare's Iago opens his mouth to speak, we know something evil will spew forth. And when Voldemort appears embodied before Harry Potter, we know that dark magic will soon follow. Academic arguments over whether this character is *the* Satan of all of Scripture (as most Christian theologians have believed for most of church history[9]) or just *a* satan/adversary (perhaps the more common view among contemporary scholars) blur when the story is read dramatically.

Satan is the villain of this story, and he is God's to deal with. It is therefore God who confronts Satan with a direct question: "Where have you come from?" (1:7).

Whenever God asks a question, it's for the benefit of someone else; he already knows the answer. In this case, the question is probably meant to create revelation in the hearts of the "sons of God" and in the hearts of those hearing the story of Job. That revelation comes in the form of Satan's answer: "From roaming throughout the earth, going back and forth on it" (1:7).

It's a mistake to take this answer, or any satanic answer, at face value. He is a liar. Which means we must consider the dramatic context of his words. Satan has come *with God's sons*. And even God's spiritual sons—translated by the NIV as "angels"—don't have unlimited authority over creation. Instead, at least some of them have been given *limited* authority over specific geographical locations.[10] So when Satan says that he comes from "roaming throughout the earth" and "going back and forth on it," he's probably boasting of his usurped authority over the earth or over its human kingdoms. He is also being belligerent and evasive.

GOD: Where have you come from?
SATAN: Anywhere I want!

What makes this a revelation is that through it Satan demonstrates the contrast between his own nature and God's. God asks a direct question. Satan answers with pride and deception. The sons of God are now witnesses, a fact that's highlighted next when God reveals what Satan has temporarily avoided saying.

Unfortunately, the next verse is often translated as, "Have you considered my servant Job?" That makes it sound as if God is the one starting this fight. More than one commentary has made the point that this confrontation was God's idea. But the dramatic implication here is that Satan came to this family dinner with a specific accusation in mind. In fact, Young's Literal Translation phrases God's question like this: "Hast thou set thy heart against My servant Job because there is none like him in the land, a man perfect and upright, fearing God, and turning aside from evil?" (1:8).

God knows where Satan has been and what he has been planning, and this question is a way of revealing the truth to those watching.

The Lie That God Only Rules by Power

What follows is perhaps the most important line in the book and is the contextual key not just to the story of Job but to much of the Bible. Satan answers, "Does Job fear God for nothing?" (1:9).

This question isn't just an accusation against Job. It's an accusation against God himself. Job isn't the primary target. This isn't about whether a person can be good or not. It's about whether God's authority is based on his power or on his character and principles.

In saying that Job is only loyal to God because of God's protection and blessing, Satan is saying—in front of the other sons of God—that the Creator of the universe rules only by power. God is not God because he is good but because he is strong. And, presumably, how is that any different from what Satan claims for himself?

Understanding this accusation is vital to understanding the story. In suggesting that God only rules by power, Satan has effectively stripped God of using his power to support or protect Job. The very accusation creates a dilemma, leaving God only three possible responses:

1. *God could simply crush Satan under the divine fist.* This is what we wish he would do because we're on Job's side. But this inclination—our desire to counter falsehood with force—only serves to prove Satan's point, that humans are allied to power, not principle. More importantly, if God does this, he will be giving credence to the accusation. Crushing Satan would only solve the problem of Satan; it wouldn't solve the problem of his reverberating lie.

2. *God could ignore the accusation.* Some might argue that God should do nothing, that his greatness—if it is really so great—shouldn't be threatened by anything. But this response fails to consider the widening circle of damage such lies create. No one really believes, when watching *Othello*, that the villain Iago can simply be ignored. Satan's lie here in Job is every bit as powerful as the one in the garden of Eden: *Has God really said . . . ?* It must be dealt with or its ripple effects will spread. Better to refute it at its source—for the sake of his "sons" and of all creation.

3. *God can let the accusation be refuted by Job.* Which is to say that God can accept the challenge in order for the lie to be defeated. He can withdraw his power and

allow principle to stand on its own, naked in the face of a horrifying evil.

The third option is the only viable one, since it is the only one capable of revealing the satanic lie as false. Unfortunately, the struggle will involve an enormous amount of human pain. In this sense, Job will become a champion for principle, for the character of God, and for the nature of the conflict between good and evil. In his own way, Job is more gallant than a knight rising to defend a lady's honor, for Job cannot strike back and is unaware of the nature of the battle he's being called to.

Satanic Authority

This setup is pure thematic storytelling. It gives evil due credit for ingenuity and twisted cleverness. But it also establishes the oppositional strength of real goodness, which lies not in the abilities of a superhero or the talents of a gifted protagonist but in moral purity and integrity of character—in what we might call virtue.

In choosing the third option, God's nature is further demonstrated when he refuses to be the agent of satanic suffering. He won't strike Job, but he will withdraw his power from the board. This fact isn't a way for God to wash his hands of his involvement; rather, it's the beginning of a revelation concerning his core nature—his "ways." Satan is holding a usurped authority over the earth, so God withdrawing his protective power will leave Satan free to bring out his cruelest torments. It's not God but Satan who afflicts Job:

> "Have you not put a hedge around him . . . ? You have blessed the work of his hands. . . . But now stretch out your hand and strike everything he has, and he will surely curse you to your face."

117

The LORD said to Satan, "Very well, then, everything he has is in your power, but on the man himself do not lay a finger." (1:10–12)

Authority thus forms the contextual backdrop for a reality of which Job's life is merely a microcosm. Some might object that God should be able to remove satanic authority as well as any possibility of widening falsehoods on the simple basis that he is God. Why doesn't he just take back the dominion Satan enjoys, regardless of whether or not it was given to him by God or Adam and Eve?[11]

But this question is another way of appealing to God's power to avoid dealing with his nature as the Unchanging One who cannot deny himself. Whatever we imagine God capable of, the story of Job is describing a conflict involving beings with real characteristics and traits that must not be dismissed arbitrarily. Satan's authority originated with God. Removing that authority requires the violation of its original terms, otherwise Satan's lie here in Job is magnified. Indeed, his lie may be intended to create just this situation. So the ultimate refutation of Satan's claim that power is greater than principle must be played out in an environment where both principle and power are allowed to collide freely.

With this challenge, then, Satan has removed what he sees as his primary obstacle: God's manifest power. Power will now be the exclusive purview of the satanic kingdom, at least in terms of this particular conflict over the afflictions of Job. Power is, after all, Satan's defining external trait.

What follows are four satanic attacks in which Job's servants are killed, his livestock are stolen, and all ten of his children die during a feast when the oldest brother's house collapses. These calamities are reported by messengers who describe (1) an attack by Sabeans, (2) fire falling from the sky, (3) Chaldean raiding parties, and (4) a mighty wind that strikes the four corners of the eldest brother's house.

These details are evidence for the first of the three literary devices mentioned earlier. *What happens on earth is a reflection of what has already happened in heaven.* Job has been turned over to Satan, with the limitation that the man himself not be harmed.[12]

Notice that the activity of Satan is manifested here through both human agents (Sabeans and Chaldeans) and natural phenomena (sky-fire and wind). Note also that it's a *human messenger* who calls this fire from the sky the "fire of God." The narrator makes no such claim. Instead, these words may be intended to turn Job's heart against God. Later we will see the same thing repeated, with Satan's prosecutor accusing God of the very things Satan himself is orchestrating.

In spite of all this suffering, we're told at the end of chapter 1, "In all this, Job did not sin by charging God with wrongdoing" (v. 22).

But Satan isn't finished yet, and in the next chapter we're taken back into the divine presence to hear the Adversary expand his previous lie from one man to all of humanity. The reason Job didn't break, Satan argues, is that humans are inherently selfish; their allegiance is ultimately to their own flesh: "But now stretch out your hand and strike his flesh and bones, and he will surely curse you to your face" (2:5).

Again God defers, withdrawing his protection further. Job's *body* is in Satan's hands, but again *his life must be spared.*

It is Satan, not God, who afflicts Job with "painful sores from the soles of his feet to the crown of his head" (2:7). Only now does Job's wife add her famously biting rebuke, "Curse God and die!"—leaving Job alone in his torment. Once again, Satan's afflictions have come through both natural phenomena and human agency.[13]

Job has become the embodiment of a story pattern that's built on the fabric of reality. The question at stake for Job is the question all of us must answer at some point: Will we love principle more than power? Or, again, is God good if he isn't good to *me*?

Satan's answer is that all humans are ultimately allied to power, even in the midst of our worship services and quiet devotionals. His accusation is "Skin for skin!" And he seems to be right—at least most of the time.

The All-Principled One

The church has historically envisioned God in three attributes of extreme power: *omniscience*, *omnipresence*, and *omnipotence*. While these conceptions are true, they're primarily inferences. They don't derive from our experience of the world or from our experience of God in the world. We know God is everywhere, but do we really *experience* him everywhere? We believe he is all-knowing, but do we *behave* as if he's all-knowing? And we confess that he holds all power in his hands, but do we really see the power brokers of this world building God's kingdom? Or do those with the money and the microphones use their resources to satisfy their own desires and oppress anyone who opposes them?

In this world the naked power of politics and prosperity is mostly concentrated in the coffers of Babylon. Wealth and influence do not generally flow to those with the highest ideals and uncorrupted virtues. Rather, power reaches its apex in the hands of those with no scruples against using it.

In short, the context of creation under the curse of satanic dominion was a disconnection of power and principle. With Satan at the helm, all power would break loose, unmoored from any controlling ethic, creative restraint, or holy objective.

This doesn't mean God isn't powerful. But the book of Job is trying to show us a reality we can't see with eyes clouded by lust for power. We want God to be powerful because our allegiance is to power, and we want to call what we love *God*. We don't want God to be principled, because we know we don't live by principle. And God's standards are as pure and uncompromising as the sun. So we call God *omnipotent* when we should be proclaiming him *omniprincipiati*, the All-Principled One.

In his book *The End of Christendom*, Malcolm Muggeridge recounts an interview he conducted with Anatoly Kuznetsov, a Russian science fiction writer who had defected to the UK during the Cold War. Muggeridge had lived in Moscow for several years and witnessed the oppression of the Russian church firsthand.

> If when I was a young correspondent in Moscow in the early thirties you had said to me that it would be possible for the Soviet regime to continue for sixty years with its policy of doing everything possible to extirpate the Christian faith, to discredit its record and its originator, and that after this there would emerge figures like Solzhenitsyn speaking the authentic language of the Christian, grasping such great Christian truths as the cross in a way that few people do in our time, I would have said, "No, it's impossible, it can't be." But I would have been wrong.[14]

What then, Muggeridge asks, is the source of the Russian church's great flourishing in a place where it should have been destroyed utterly? Kuznetsov answers:

> If in this world you are confronted with absolute power, power unmitigated, unrestrained, extending to every area of human life—if you are confronted with power in those terms, you are driven to realize that the only possible response to it is not some alternative power arrangement, more humane, more enlightened. The only possible response to absolute power is the absolute love which our Lord brought into the world.[15]

During the Cold War the Russian church refused to pit their own pitiful power against the vast and unrestrained power of the Soviet empire. Instead, they turned to principle, the real "power" of God that reveals his true nature. God *is* love.

Or consider what happened in Beijing on June 5, 1989, when Chinese tanks rolled into Tiananmen Square to crush a student protest. One unidentified man carrying a bag of groceries stopped in front of that line of tanks and refused to move. Western cameras caught the image and spread it across the globe. Here was a David and Goliath moment where David didn't even have a sling. Principle in the form of one man's naked courage stared down power embodied in a rolling line of Type 59 main battle tanks. And principle won.

That, ultimately, is the message of Job we have such a hard time believing. But Job did believe it. Even when he had good reason not to.

At the end of chapter 2 we are told that Job's suffering is so great it draws the attention of his three friends, Eliphaz, Bildad, and Zophar. They arrive to comfort him in his pain and grief but are so overwhelmed by the magnitude of his afflictions that they merely sit with him for a week, saying nothing.

Job's Friends

Here is where the opening frame ends and the book's inner, earthly sections begin. A comprehensive review of these middle chapters would likely not help us understand how Job establishes context for God's story. Nevertheless, it's worth pausing briefly to unpack the main function of chapters 3–27, which present a debate over the cause of Job's suffering, with Job alone defending his integrity and his three friends taking turns trying to convince him to repent.

The gist of the friends' arguments is that God uses power against the wicked,[16] so Job *must* be wicked or he wouldn't be

122

suffering. Eliphaz, Bildad, and Zophar make increasingly harsh accusations throughout this section as Job refuses to accept their advice and admit to crimes he hasn't committed.

Job's response to their deterministic logic strikes at the core of their humanity: "You see something dreadful and are afraid. . . . My integrity is at stake" (6:21, 29). His friends are terrified that the universe may not be ruled by a God who punishes the wicked and rewards the righteous. They need to believe in a universe governed by absolute justice, even if that belief isn't mirrored in reality—even if their belief causes Job additional pain.

Ironically, their arguments aren't uncommon in the church. We have a tendency to oversimplify suffering, and the book of Job takes its time in addressing the emotional damage such dismissive attitudes can cause.

It is possible, perhaps even likely, that the book is doing something else here as well, something revealed through its narrative device of reflection. However, the function of this initial dialogue between the four men will be best understood later.

Elihu: Whose God Is He?

After the authorial comment of chapter 28,[17] Job continues his lament for three chapters, ending with a final appeal to his own innocence. He is answered in chapter 32 not by any of his three friends, who have "stopped answering Job, because he was righteous in his own eyes" (v. 1) but by a new character who has apparently been listening to this lengthy exchange all along:

> But Elihu son of Barakel the Buzite, of the family of Ram, became very angry with Job for justifying himself rather than God. He was also angry with the three friends, because they had found no way to refute Job, and yet had condemned him. (vv. 2–3)

At this point the story's chiastic structure points to Elihu as a counterpart to Job's friends, except that Elihu hasn't been named as one of them, has appeared suddenly out of nowhere, and shows no signs of friendship. In fact, almost immediately Elihu demonstrates not just a complete lack of empathy but a hostility that can only be justified in the text by his youthful zeal (32:18–21). It's likely, therefore, that his placement here is initially intended to mirror the function of Job's friends as his accusers.[18]

Scholars have attributed various roles to Elihu, including that of scribe, divine advocate, and heavenly prosecutor. These are hard to support from a dramatic perspective. Furthermore, they all seem to miss the real timbre of Elihu's words. If we don't feel the sting of this young man's arrogance and cruelty, it probably means we haven't fully empathized with Job's deep anguish of soul and physical torment.

Imagine you've just lost all ten of your children. Your life savings has been stolen and your business burned to the ground. There's no insurance, so there will be no rebuilding, no replacement of your lost income or wealth. Worse, your physical body is suddenly covered in boils that may indicate syphilis, leprosy, or something even worse.[19] And now your best friends are publicly accusing you of terrible wickedness based only on their assumption that you *must* be guilty because otherwise you wouldn't be getting what you deserved.

After all this, a nineteen-year-old zealot claiming to speak for God—a seminary student perhaps—demands that you listen to him because God has given him knowledge of right and wrong (32:9), plus he was born with extraordinary understanding (32:8). Also, he has a right to speak to you however he wants because he has very strong feelings (32:19) and his words "come from an upright heart" (33:3). Listen up, old man, and Elihu will teach you wisdom (33:33)!

> For the ear tests words
>> as the tongue tastes food.
>> *Let us discern for ourselves what is right;*
>> let us learn together what is good. (34:3–4, emphasis
>> added)

That line in verse 4 should set off alarm bells. Elihu is echo-ing the serpent's lie in the garden of Eden. Elihu is not a divine prosecutor but a devilish one.[20]

Furthermore, we must understand that the dramatic tension of this story doesn't lie primarily in the opening chapters. Satan's early gambits are only a prelude to something worse. The story doesn't bleed away its tension through a slow processing of Job's misery. It builds in intensity as the first hammer blows of disaster give way to more precise calculations of torture.

Job is still suffering here in the confrontation with Elihu. He isn't looking back on his pain; his pain is all around him. He still carries the boils and the grief and the bewilderment. From his perspective, the agonies are all happening now. The story, in other words, isn't over. Its tension isn't gone. Everything in Job's life is getting *worse*.

If we miss this, we will miss the dramatic significance of chapters 3–38. What happens after the first two chapters of Job—the bulk of the story—isn't the aftermath of Job's pain but its dramatic climax. And like any good storyteller, the author of Job has saved the most terrible confrontation for last.

Elihu is a tool for Satan's last temptation. He is a mouth-piece for the Adversary, who is even now using him to try to break Job in the darkest moment of his life. And he does so through a lengthy series of accusations against both Job and God, each of which is best understood in light of Elihu's role as a satanic accuser. In spirit, Elihu is a medieval torturer bend-ing over his racked victim and demanding submission to the new king:

Since God cannot do wrong, the wrongdoer must be Job. (34:10–12)

God will not let you have your day in court. (34:23)

You sinned openly, so God is punishing you openly. (34:26–28)

Why would God reward you with relief when you refuse to repent? (34:33)

If only God would cause you to suffer more! (34:36)

Job, you are rebelling against the God of power! (34:37)

God is unaffected by the good and evil done on earth. (35:8)

God does not answer when people cry out. (35:12–13)

Why would God listen to you when everything you say is empty? (35:16)

My words can't be false because I am perfect in knowledge. (36:3–4)

If you will just repent and thereby agree with my argument, your torment will cease. (36:11)

You are evil and would rather stay evil than get relief from your suffering! (36:17–21)

God is exalted in his power. Power is how he governs. The Almighty is beyond our reach and exalted in power. (36:22; 36:27–31; 37:23)

Whose God is he? Mine. He is *my* God, Elihu's God, the God of power.

The irony here is that Elihu is correct. His god *is* a god of power. But his god isn't the God of the opening frame, not the God Job has been appealing to. His god isn't God. His god is Leviathan, the "king over all who are proud" (41:34).

Satan is still at work in this story, still acting through human agents, and his selection of a young man filled with emotion and self-righteousness and religious zeal is the perfect choice for exacting the most agonizing existential torment from Job.

It's also significant that, as Robert Alter points out, the poetry of Elihu is "vastly inferior" to everything else in the book.[21] In fact, it represents a deliberate contrast with the poetry of God in chapters 38–41. While contemporary scholars, including Alter, attribute this disparity to the Elihu chapters possibly being later additions, it's more likely an artistic flourish of characterization. Good storytellers create distinction in their characters' dialogue. That Elihu's poetry is bad is to be expected. His artistry is as malformed as his theology.

Furthermore, none of Elihu's thirty different references to God is the personal name Yahweh (YHWH)—an omission Stephen Vicchio puts down to Elihu's "divine plan" theology.[22] But again, a more direct explanation seems likely. Elihu is mirroring the Adversary in the opening chapters, who similarly calls God only by his universal name.

Still, the most striking thing in these chapters is what Elihu *does* say. His arrogance and cruelty are breathtaking. If anything could push Job away from God, it would be this. If anything could tempt Job to compromise his integrity, it would be a youthful prosecutor in a clerical collar, appearing just in time to defend God against Job's wickedness.

Dramatically, this interpretation is demonstrated in the way the scene acts as yet another reflection of what came before: Job's council of friends is a mirror image of God's divine council of spirit-sons. Just as God has been figuratively stripped of power by Satan's lie, so has Job been stripped of power by Satan's hand. Just as God has been accused by the Adversary, so Job is accused by the Adversary's agents. What happens on earth has already happened in heaven: "One day the sons of God came to present themselves before the LORD, and Satan also came with them" (1:6). And one day the friends of Job came to present themselves before Job, and Elihu also came with them.

This reflection is now revealed as a mirror not just of what we have already seen but of what we can't see as earthbound creatures. If Job's friends are reflections of the "sons of God," are their accusations echoes of discontent in the divine presence?

This question is worth asking, even though a definite answer is impossible. We're not told directly what the sons of God might be saying. All we have are the words of Eliphaz, Bildad, and Zophar. We hear through a glass darkly. But we do hear. And what we hear may not be uniquely human.

From Job's perspective there's only one response to Elihu's false accusations and only one answer to his demands for a compromise.

Job ignores him.

And God ignores him.

But the Lord answers Job.

Darkening God's Counsel

And so we come to God's answer—if you can call it that—which he delivers out of a storm. God is heard but not seen. The Lord is concealed, a disembodied voice that speaks not to Elihu or (for the time being) to Job's friends, but to Job himself.

His answers are mostly questions, beginning with, "Who is this that obscures my plans with words without knowledge?" (38:2).

G. K. Chesterton says that God has opened court with a very procedural question: he is effectively saying, "State your name for the record."[23] But it is the phrasing of his question that inspires my imagination. In his ignorance, Job has obscured God's plans, or, more literally, *darkened God's counsel*. His words have mischaracterized God's true nature as far less beautiful and glorious than God really is.

Two chapters of such detailed questions are enough to show Job that he hasn't really known or understood God's nature. What he has known in theory from a distance is so far exceeded by God's reality that Job is left nearly speechless (40:4–5). But God isn't finished with his cross-examination.

"Would you discredit my justice? Would you condemn me to justify yourself?" (40:8). This seems to be the critical point, for it addresses a flaw common to humans throughout history. When life causes us to ask, "Is God still good if he is not good to *me*?" most of us answer, "No!" Because we measure the universe by the moral standard of our own preferences and comfort, any God that doesn't serve our perceived self-interest cannot be trusted and cannot be good. So we make assumptions about the nature of life, the nature of the world, and even the nature of the spirit realm. We darken God's counsel with words without knowledge. This tendency is probably what God is addressing when he points Job to the two creatures of chapters 40–41, Behemoth and Leviathan.

Perhaps no aspect of the book of Job has been interpreted more wildly than these two enigmatic beasts. Creationists have linked the traits of these creatures to dinosaurs. Greg Boyd places them together in the camp of mythical chaos creatures.[24] Scientist Hugh Ross follows the more traditional interpretation popularly noted in study Bibles and says Behemoth was probably a hippopotamus and Leviathan a crocodile.[25] Others have claimed that, whatever their identity, their fearsomeness renders them embodiments of God's sovereign power—so what God must be saying here is that if Job can't stand before the power of Behemoth and Leviathan, what business does he have slinging accusations at their Maker?

None of these interpretations accounts for the dramatic chiastic structure of the story or fully explains the extraordinary contradictions of their differing traits. Behemoth is nothing like Leviathan. These creatures are not twins. They aren't even complementary examples of God's power. Instead, Behemoth and Leviathan are *contrasting* visions of ultimate reality.

Unraveling their significance requires use of the second and third literary devices, chiasmus and layered meaning. For starters, notice how the presence of God, the "sons of God," and Satan in (B) are mirrored in (B').

A Job and God | Sacrifice, Household
  B God, Sons, and Satan | Confrontation
    C Job and Friends | Temptation
      D Interlude | Wisdom and the Fear of the Lord
    C' Job and Elihu | Temptation
  B' God, Job, and Leviathan | Confrontation
A' Job and God | Restoration, Household

Scholars have long pointed out that Satan seems to disappear after chapter 2. But, as we saw with the young Elihu, Satan doesn't disappear. He is merely reflected.

Reflection is necessary here not to hide Satan but to honor the image of the unimaginable God of creation. God cannot be expressed adequately in creation. It would be unthinkable for the author of Job to attempt to conjure an image of the Almighty. Until Christ, the best any storyteller could do was point to creation itself and say, "That tree, that mountain, those stars—all are shouting the glory of God!" This is why God does not tell Job, "Look at me!" but instead says, "Look at Behemoth. . . . It ranks first among the works of God" (40:15, 19). *Works* here can also be translated as *ways*.

Behemoth, then, is not God. It is a beginning of the works and the ways of God. And each of God's comments about Behemoth's nature (40:15–24) is designed as a riddle that must be unpacked thoughtfully in order to see its literal, typological, and metaphorical contents. Behemoth is not just a hippo; it is also the earth (as distinct from the sea) and a representative expression of God's ways.

Leviathan, on the other hand, is not just a thrashing sea monster. Typologically, it is the sea as the embodiment of chaos. Metaphorically, it is a representation of Satan and his externalized power. Leviathan "looks down on all that are haughty; it is king over all that are proud" (41:34).

Behold a Wonderful Hippo!

It is structurally significant that Job's concluding answer to God follows this contrasting revelation of Behemoth and Leviathan. In fact, Job repeats God's initial question before answering:

> You asked, "Who is this that obscures my plans
>   without knowledge?"
> Surely I spoke of things I did not understand,
>   things too wonderful for me to know. . . .
> My ears had heard of you
>   but now my eyes have seen you.
> Therefore I despise myself [or "it"]
>   and repent in dust and ashes. (42:3, 5–6)

Now my eyes have seen you—but how? Has the narrator forgotten to mention this supreme encounter? Or are we meant to understand that in seeing God's creation—God's *works* and God's *ways*—Job has indeed seen the Lord in the only sense that any human possibly could?

Are we meant to realize that Job has beheld a truly wonderful hippo—earth as it is meant to be, restored to the control of the only one who is worthy to rule it, the one whose sovereignty is not based in power? The one who, when passing before Moses, described himself in terms not of power but of positive ideals—indeed, of *relational* ideals: "The LORD, the LORD, the compassionate and gracious God, slow to anger, abounding in love and faithfulness, maintaining love to thousands, and forgiving wickedness, rebellion and sin. Yet he does not leave the guilty unpunished" (Exod. 34:6–7).

The book of Job is the essential context of Scripture. It forms a spiritual backdrop of history from Eden to Golgotha. Its great significance lies in its dramatic unveiling of the divine conflict that has shaped the affairs of earth.

Will we choose power, or will we choose principle? That is the question we must answer on our way to meeting God. It is the question that has been asked of every person of God, every follower of Jesus, from Adam and Eve to the end of the age. And every person except Jesus has answered it wrongly at some point. Every patriarch, every saint, every human icon of biblical virtue has failed. Power has corrupted, and devout power has corrupted devoutly.

We have all believed the lie that we would use power for good if only we had the chance. But when we are given that chance, we sooner or later prove our claim to be false and our allegiance to goodness exaggerated. The very best of us eventually fail, a fact to which the entire Old Testament is a monument:

Joseph delivered the ancient world from famine, then "reduced the people to servitude, from one end of Egypt to the other" (Gen. 47:21).

Gideon delivered Israel through faith, then built an idol from the profits of his own greed (Judg. 8:27).

Elijah called all Israel to repentance, then killed a hundred soldiers with the power of supernatural fire (2 Kings 1:10–12). (Clearly, Jesus didn't approve; see Luke 9:54–55.)

Even **Moses,** the man who most ably represented the
authority and power of God to the world, ultimately
failed to do so accurately (Num. 20:7–12).

The list could go on and on, but why bother? It wasn't just
Moses who struck the rock. We've *all* struck the rock! We've all
sold out and built idols and called down fire on our enemies.
And most of us did so not because someone held a gun to our
head or offered us a billion-dollar contract. We have sold out
far more cheaply—for convenience, for comfort, for a delusion
of self-righteousness.

Thankfully, God's kingdom isn't ushered in through power.
It's ushered in through principle, through the relational ideals
that lie at the heart of the language of story,[26] the ideals that
point to a God who knows and wants to be known.

All of Scripture shouts this. But these shouts are God-shouts,
which means they're loud like a sunrise. They're subtle even in
their insistence; revealed best through a still, small voice rather
than a wind, earthquake, or fire (1 Kings 19:11–12). The God-
shouts of Scripture speak peace to the storm (Luke 8:24) and
truth to every power (Matt. 26:64–65). They are truly wonderful
in their hippo-ness. And once you see them hiding under the
lotus, you cannot unsee them, nor do you want to.

From Zechariah's startling declaration, "'Not by might
nor by power, but by my Spirit,' says the LORD Almighty"
(Zech. 4:6), to Paul's revelation from Jesus that "my power is
made perfect in weakness" (2 Cor. 12:9), the Bible is setting
the stage for a great revealing of Christ as the All-Principled
One.

Someday the angels and the people of earth will rejoice that
Jesus has finally (finally!) taken his power and begun to reign
(Rev. 11:17). And we will all join together to celebrate and
proclaim, "You are worthy, our Lord and God, to receive glory
and honor and power" (4:11).

The God of Ubuntu

Yet there remains one more glimpse behind the curtain that must be addressed in order to understand—or at least to not misunderstand—the story of Job.

If "now my eyes have seen you" is pointing to Behemoth as a typological and metaphorical representation of God's works and God's ways, then Behemoth is more than a wonderful hippo; it is the earth Christ will one day return to, both in power and embodying the underlying principles by which he governs the cosmos.

But Behemoth must not be mistaken for God himself. Otherwise we fall into the same error Job's friends did and end up aligning not with the Creator but with a list of attributes. This is surely not what the writer of Job intended. Such might be "wisdom," but it isn't what Job has asked for.

I won't say that this is the revelatory interpretation of the book of Job. Yet I will point out that what should be the most obvious dramatic point made by the story is one that is almost always overlooked as a mere structural convenience.

God meets with Job.

Here at the end of the story Job finally gets what he's been asking for—an audience with the living God. None of his friends have asked for or even wanted such an audience. Elihu has denied that such a meeting would even be possible. In fact, the only person in this story who seeks a relationship with God is its eponymous hero.

Job has been wrong about God, placing blame where none exists. He has fumed, lamented, and even accused the Creator, but he hasn't walked away. He hasn't given up. He has continued to relate to God even under the most extreme duress. It may be hurtful to scream and yell, but screaming and yelling are signs of connection. A strained relationship is, after all, still a relationship.

This relational quality in the story is perhaps its most important revelation, for it isn't focused on a single man or even on humanity. Instead, the climax of the story is a meeting—a conversation—between Job and Yahweh concerning the nature of God as "God" (Elohim; see Job 40:1–2). Yahweh speaks to Job as a person. He is not a mere collection of attributes. The point isn't that God is the true north of our moral compass and the fixed standard of our story ideals. What matters here at the end is that Yahweh is a person Job is invited to know. God's relational nature is the common thread of every positive ideal, of every principle.

This too is mirrored in the story at its very end as the storm clouds literally and figuratively disappear. Job's property is returned to him, and his wealth is doubled in all but one category. Where he had seven thousand sheep at the beginning, at the end he has fourteen thousand. His lost camels, three thousand in number, are in the end replaced by six thousand. And his oxen and donkeys are similarly doubled.

The oddity of this doubling lies in the strange fact that Job, who has lost ten children to death, is given ten, not twenty, more. Furthermore, of the ten new children only three are named— Job's daughters: Jemimah, Keziah, and Karen-Happuch. The males are not named. Both of these facts are startling reversals of our expectations. Whenever a story upends the normative we can be sure it is trying to tell us something.

Job's reward has indeed doubled, for the ultimate destiny of God's people isn't finite but eternal. Job's lost children won't remain lost. He will see them again, and when he does, when the story draws its final curtain closed, Job will count not ten children but twenty.

Here at last is where the story of Christ comes most into focus for anyone with eyes to see and ears to hear. G. K. Chesterton came close to spelling it out:

> But in the prologue we see Job tormented not because he was the worst of men, but because he was the best. . . . I need not suggest what a high and strange history awaited this paradox

135

of the best man in the worst fortune. I need not say that in the freest and most philosophical sense there is one Old Testament figure who is truly a type; or say what is prefigured in the wounds of Job.[27]

It's no accident that the book of Job ends with a feast, with Job's family and friends giving him silver and gold, with the naming of daughters and the restoration of his kingdom.[28] The best stories, the truest stories, aren't the ones that end in misery but the ones that remind us of the restoration of all things— and the goodness of the God who has promised to make our suffering both meaningful and temporary.

"And so Job died, an old man and full of years" (42:17).

So ends the book of Job.

But the story of Job goes on.

CHARACTERIZATION

7

KILL THE WABBIT!

A story's central character is called the *protagonist* or, more colloquially, the *hero*. What makes this central figure important is her role as the moral center of the tale. As important as the ideals of any story are, they can only work dramatically if they are embodied—incarnated, if you will—in the actions and decisions of fictional people. "You cannot tell a story about a gun," my writing mentor, science fiction author James Gunn, used to say, "but you can tell a story about a man with a gun."

The central figure of any story must be a person. Whoever that is, he or she is uniquely positioned to embody the audience's projection of the self. What she wants, we want. What she fears, we fear. As she succeeds or fails, so do we.

Because fictional characters are not real people but only representations, the language of story draws protagonists on two coexisting planes—two accessible selves. One is the character's *internal* identity; the other is their *external* identity. Not every story explores these selves equally, but the default standard for a fictional protagonist—the universal template, if you will—is based on the conjunction of the inner and outer. Story, in other words, seems to view even individual human beings through a contextual lens of parallelism.

It's not difficult to see why. Personality is the ultimate expression of personhood, and the simplest way to express the complexity of a human being is in a place of conjoined selves.

In life we experience our own inner and outer selves almost constantly. But we only ever experience the external selves of others. The inner life of someone else can only be known vicariously and imperfectly through something like a novel or memoir. But the external life of strangers is always present: we cheer for friends and family as they navigate life; we embrace the ups and downs of colleagues and peers as they celebrate or grieve; we follow the public lives of politicians and actors and despots via the nightly news.

The protagonist is therefore a mechanism for experiencing classes or types of experiences (Diana Wynne Jones's "mental maps") that we could not otherwise have. When the hero embarks on some adventure of discovery or revenge or restoration, we easily recognize that external struggle as a natural part of life. And when the hero is forced by story events to confront some internal flaw, we recognize that battle of repentance—the inner conflict of *who we will be*—as universal. Combined, these inner and outer struggles form the core of someone we can identify with.

This is how the protagonist becomes the central viewpoint through which story events are interpreted. It is why, for any story to resolve, the hero must overcome an outer force of opposition and an inner force of conflicting desires.

The Inner Self

Conflicting desires are dramatically illustrated through moral growth, which is why protagonists are almost always flawed.

A moral flaw gives the character room to grow—and the story a way to resolve. Without a flaw, or at least a temptation, the character can't change. And if the character has no room to change and grow, the story's middle section won't produce a feeling of increasing tension. It will be a boring pause.

This doesn't mean the protagonist's flaw must be tragic or even large. Minor flaws can be effective in stories because, as in life, they often have big consequences. Little lies can produce huge problems, creating a ripple effect that moves outward from one person to their family, friends, and community.

The job of the storyteller is to extrapolate the effects of such flaws even when they're minor. Great storytellers show us how the tiniest of sins can have devastating effects on others. "Let our artists rather be those," Plato wrote, "who are gifted to discern the true nature of the beautiful and graceful."[1]

It's a Wonderful Life, the classic Christmas movie starring Jimmy Stewart, is an iconic example of this. The protagonist, George Bailey, doesn't start out as a bad person. He starts out as a good person, a man who is self-sacrificing and kind and humble and courageous. But George believes a lie. And the lie he believes is something lots of people agree with, even if we don't admit it out loud. It's one of those things we believe privately but never verbalize because to speak it aloud would sound ugly and hedonistic.

George Bailey believes that the best possible life is the sort spent in travel and completing great projects. He believes in making his mark on the world by building bridges and seeing the wonders of history and perhaps winning a medal of honor fighting Nazis. He thinks that big men do big things.

The movie is a thoughtful examination of why that idea is wrong. It shows George, and therefore the audience, that the ordinary life he has lived is actually the remarkable one. No, he didn't go to war. He didn't even go to college. All he did was help common people in the miserable backwater town of Bedford Falls.

Along the way, the story (as all great stories do) exerts pressure on the hero to believe its core lie. When George pushes toward greatness, the story pushes back. At a crucial point, George says, "I suppose everyone would be better off if I'd never been born," and Clarence the angel says, "All right, you've got your wish." The rest of the film is a slow unpacking of the ripple effect of that little lie.

What makes this story work is that we don't expect the lie to extend as far as it does. The magnitude of the lie is shocking. And the reason it's shocking is that we believe the lie too.

It's not until the movie resolves and George says, "Take me back, Clarence. I want to live again," that he is made whole. In renouncing the lie, George Bailey becomes more than a good man; he becomes a great man. And it happens because of the pressure generated during the middle section of the story, which is designed to expose the lie for what it is. George Bailey's growth—and the subsequent revelation of the lie shared by protagonist and audience—wouldn't be possible if George didn't start out believing something seemingly innocuous.

The principle of internal characterization, then, is that a protagonist's private/inner self is revealed through growth demonstrated by the correction of a flaw. For a story to end well, the hero must fix his inner brokenness through repentance.

The Outer Self

It's not just the inner life of the main character that demonstrates growth. The protagonist's outer self also matters. This part of his or her identity will, in story terms, be defined by the problem/solution pattern sometimes called the *story goal*. A story goal is the thing the protagonist is working to achieve, and it will only be effective if the desire to achieve it is shared by the audience. Frodo Baggins, for instance, wants to destroy the One Ring, and we who have traveled Middle-earth by his side are emotionally invested in his success. Likewise, it is not just Luke Skywalker who wants to see the Death Star destroyed, or Dorothy who wants to find her way home from Oz. Each of these characters is driven by a desire to achieve something outside of themselves. They seek to change some aspect of their world—or, in Dorothy's case, to change worlds altogether.

Story goals are typically analyzed in terms of plot, but it's important to understand how they shape our perception of the main character. Truly immersive narratives connect us so deeply to the protagonist's outer motivation that we tend to judge every event, character, or setback by its impact on the story goal. When reading or watching a performance of *Romeo and Juliet*, for instance, our emotions are filtered through the viewpoint of the teenaged lovers, not that of their disapproving parents.

This bonding effect is so strong that audiences can be drawn to cheer for those who would, in most other circumstances, be seen as criminals. Think Michael Corleone in *The Godfather* movies or, more recently, Katniss Everdeen in *The Hunger Games*. Once an audience is centered in the viewpoint of the protagonist, we can't help interpreting every event through the bias of vicarious self-interest (a.k.a. the tree of the knowledge of good and evil).

But even as story obstacles are inevitably seen through this lens, so too is the protagonist's outer self defined by the obstacles he or she overcomes. In a good story, these usually create a certain amount of physical and emotional torment. Sure, the heroine may get what she wants in the end, but along the way it's going to hurt—a *lot*. Hercules wouldn't be a true hero had his labors included, say, taking out the trash and washing the dishes. Frodo's journey wouldn't be interesting or enlightening if he'd caught a ride to Mordor on the back of a giant eagle. And Dorothy needed to journey through Oz in order to appreciate the words of the Wizard at the end.

One way or another, story demands that the protagonist suffers. Why? Because suffering is the only currency by which the value of the story goal can be established.

In 1999, comedian Billy Crystal paid $239,000 for one of Mickey Mantle's baseball gloves.[2] I recall learning about it from a nightly news program, after which I muttered something like, "No glove is worth that much money!" I was wrong, of course. What made the glove so valuable is a principle of economics true of eBay and of insurance law and of all humanity: something is worth the highest price anyone is willing to pay for it.

The consequences of this principle aren't just narratively essential; they're theologically profound, setting in motion a domino effect of ultimate meaning. In stories, the only currency of any value is the emotional investment of the audience. This means that in order to create buy-in, a storyteller *must arrange for the protagonist to suffer*.

We've all read stories that ended too easily; what causes such stories to fail is a lack of value created through investment. Unless the main character suffers in some way, we have no idea what the story goal is worth. But when Luke Skywalker loses his mentor, Obi-Wan Kenobi, in the process of stealing the Death Star's blueprints, we feel the importance of his quest. When Gandalf goes over the edge of Khazad-dûm, we feel the importance of Frodo's quest—and the value of the story goal is cemented in our hearts.

For a story to end well, the hero must pay a significant price.

Emotional Resolution

The price paid by the hero is what makes the resolution of a story satisfying. Good stories make us feel things by forcing us to identify so strongly with the protagonist that their suffering becomes ours. When a story resolves at the attainment of the story goal, we feel it because we're participating in the

144

tension of the central conflict. It's not just Luke Skywalker who destroys the Death Star; every person in the audience fires that remarkable last shot.

This sort of resolution derives from a logical, true-to-life realignment of what *is* with what *should be*. Stories resolve because something that was wrong is made right. But though that resolution must fit logically within the story's dramatic situation, what it produces in the audience isn't at first rational. We don't read novels to be taught. We read them to be entertained.

Understanding the role of emotion in story is key to recognizing its power. The better a story is crafted—the more immersive and emotive it is—the more an audience will enjoy it. We love stories that move us. But we don't just love them. We surrender to them. We have no immunity against a powerful story, even when that story is communicating something that contradicts our worldview.

This has been demonstrated by research. In a paper published in the *Journal of Personality and Social Psychology*, researchers Melanie Green and Timothy Brock presented research indicating that the more transported an audience is, the more they adapt their beliefs to match those underpinning the story. They write, "Becoming involved in a narrative world seemed to have measurable consequences. Although these correlational analyses cannot establish causality, a likely possibility is that individuals altered their real-world beliefs in response to experiences in a story world."[3]

A well-told story bypasses our intellectual firewalls and changes us through our emotions. Story isn't a direct assault on our ability to reason and consider all sides. It's not an invitation for the mind to participate in a fair debate. Story is a sneaky torpedo shot aimed at the heart. Story, in other words, uses the most direct and immediate pathway to neural processing that any human has in order to help us interpret the nature of the real world.[4] It uses emotion to build a moral map of reality.

A microbiologist once asked me politely why I thought the stories-as-flight-simulators idea was too simple. I replied that it is the right-and-wrong foundation of stories that best reveals their true function. "If the point is mere survival," I asked her, "why are heroes so often required to sacrifice themselves?"

She had an excellent answer, and one I was expecting. "Maybe because the hero is sacrificing himself for someone else? For his family or tribe? In which case the Darwinian explanation holds, because what he is really protecting is his genetic blueprint."

"That would make sense," I said, "if our story patterns consistently elevated the survival of family and tribe over personal survival. But that isn't what we see. What we see in stories is the elevation of a moral standard above survival, above even the survival of one's family and friends. No one celebrates the Nazis who defended the collapsing Third Reich in its final days. We do celebrate Anne Frank's naive but beautiful optimism."

I would add here that no price is too high, no sacrifice too large, that the language of story would not demand its payment in the service of a moral absolute. Even reading "Horatius at the Bridge"—the quintessential sacrifice-for-one's-tribe story—it is clear that Macaulay is celebrating not the salvation of Rome but the courage of its gatekeeper. That Horatius held off the invading Etruscans is part of the story's happy ending. But what makes it work as a story, what gives it depth of theme, is that he was willing to pay the ultimate price for a principle. His valor would have been no less praiseworthy had he succumbed to his wounds as the bridge collapsed.

But story's commitment to a moral standard of perfection requires something besides a defining principle and an emotional reaction in the audience. In order to produce that reaction, the principle must be tested, the feelings triggered by something significant and meaningful. The guiding principle of a story won't make sense until its worth is established. Horatius certainly had the option to *not* be brave when the Etruscan army appeared on the horizon. But it was only an option because they did. Horatius could be neither coward nor hero in their absence. In their presence he could be either, and the choice was his.

> Then out spoke brave Horatius, the Captain of the
>   Gate:
> "To every man upon this earth, death cometh soon or
>   late;
> And how can man die better than facing fearful odds,
> For the ashes of his fathers, and the temples of his
>   Gods."[5]

Notice that Horatius pins his valor to a principle, not a people. *We all die. Why not die well, for something eternal and absolute?*

Such choices are essential in stories because they show us the value of an ideal in relation to reality. They reveal to us the central importance of the moral compass.

The Moral Center

Throughout history, stories have focused on the fact that the hero is flawed. This seems to be a universal observation across cultures and epochs. Gilgamesh is flawed. King David is flawed. Beowulf is flawed. This makes sense, because after you've lived awhile you realize that everyone really *is* flawed.

When it comes to stories, however, there are a few exceptions. But these exceptions exist to prove the rule. Heroes like Superman—or the clever "best of us" hero who defeats the villain through some admirable ideal—don't tell us that we're all superheroes or role models. They tell us that we *should* be. They're like recruiting posters. They work by assuming that we in the audience are flawed in a way the hero is not. The hero is a stand-in for the ideal we should all be trying to achieve.

It's important to understand that the flaw in the protagonist couldn't exist—and wouldn't work in the story to produce room for growth—if the audience didn't recognize the flaw as a real defect. The reason we feel George Bailey's despair and repentance so strongly at the end of *It's a Wonderful Life* is that we've believed the same lie. And when it's proved to be a lie, we undergo an internal emotional shift just as George Bailey does. That couldn't happen if we didn't recognize the truth of the movie. It's a truth—like all effective story themes—that appeals to something outside of our material, pragmatic impulses.

It seems the language of story can't work without an objective moral standard for human behavior—a moral compass based on something other than personal preference. Story requires a physical human component and a spiritual human component, and it requires that these work together. Whatever you call it—conscience, instinct, the soul—we can't tell a story without it. Without a ghost in the machine, story dies.

This may be one reason Jesus relied so heavily on parables and metaphors to communicate his theology. Story is tailor-made for such a conjunction of the material and nonmaterial. Kenneth Bailey writes, "Jesus was a *metaphorical* theologian. That is, his primary method of creating meaning was through metaphor, simile, parable and dramatic action rather than through logic and reasoning. He created meaning like a dramatist and a poet rather than a philosopher."[6]

This doesn't mean story is inherently religious. It does imply that we intuitively perceive the material world as linked to something intangible. In other words, stories assume a yardstick against which the hero and the audience can be measured.

A story isn't just about the protagonist—it's also about the audience. But most of all, it's about the yardstick; the hero's flaw can only exist if moral absolutes are real. Perhaps this is why the inner self is so often used to apply pressure on the character's outer self. The flaw becomes another obstacle blocking the hero's path to the story goal. Frodo isn't just opposed by orcs, goblins, Ringwraiths, and the betrayal of his friends; he's also being twisted by a growing love for the ring he plans to destroy. Near the end, the flaw that was barely noticeable at the beginning of the story has become monstrous in its power.

How any protagonist deals with the pressure created by such internal dissonance will determine whether he or she overcomes the flaw or is destroyed by it; it will also determine whether the story goal is attained. This is how the hero becomes a bridge between the yardstick—the moral compass of chapter 3—and the audience.

I'm not arguing here that morality is a set of knowable absolutes that exist outside of human preference and therefore all human behavior can be measured against them. I'm merely pointing out that *this is what story is saying*. Story, as a recurring pattern, assumes these moral absolutes really exist.

That story doesn't try to go further is significant. Theologian Allen Lewis comments on a story principle he describes as "indirect directness":

> The *directness* with which narrative approaches us is matched, therefore, by the *indirectness* with which it approaches God. In consequence, stories both acknowledge that God is beyond all description and comprehension, and yet demonstrate that God *can* be known and understood.[7]

Substitute the word *morality* for *God* and the same principle holds. Stories acknowledge moral absolutes *indirectly* by dealing with human experience *directly*.

We may not like the idea of a perfect moral yardstick. We may not agree that such a thing is real. It hardly matters. Story never builds anything substantial without a tape measure.

This leads to a more startling conclusion: you probably *do* agree with the idea of moral absolutes. If you didn't, you'd never be able to enjoy a story. When Ebenezer Scrooge is confronted by the ghosts of Christmas past, present, and future, you wouldn't be moved by his repentance. You'd think, "Why does it matter if the old ladies steal his silk shirt after he's dead? Why does it matter if Tiny Tim dies or Scrooge's nephew mocks his uncle? None of those things is wrong because good and evil are both just illusions." Nobody actually thinks this when engaged in a story. We rarely think it in real life except when we're planning something we know to be wrong.

Kill the Wabbit!

I grew up watching Warner Brothers cartoons. I still think Bugs Bunny and Road Runner are masterpieces of comedic storytelling. One of my favorites is their spoof of Wagnerian opera in which Elmer Fudd falls in love with Bugs Bunny—and then falls out of love and is driven to "kill the wabbit!"

"Kill the wabbit" is about as clear a character motivation as you can have. Clarity is one reason the Warner Brothers cartoons are so brilliant. Every cartoon tells a story so simple that anyone of any age can both understand and enjoy it. Such dramatic clarity isn't easy.

In "What's Opera, Doc?" Elmer Fudd thinks he has fallen in love with Brunhilda. But Brunhilda is really Bugs Bunny in disguise. When Bugs's helmet falls off and his long bunny ears pop out, Elmer Fudd is enraged. We know from past cartoons that Elmer Fudd's one driving desire in life is to hunt wabbits.

As simple as this is, it's pure storytelling. The hero has a desire—a story goal—that produces conflict when mixed with his moral flaw.

Elmer Fudd wants Brunhilda.

His moral flaw is that he hates bunnies.

The story will end—as good stories always do—when these two things, the internal and the external, connect in a single

moment of resolution. Either the hero attains the story goal
or he doesn't. If he *does*, it's because he overcame that moral
flaw. If he *doesn't*, it's because the flaw got the better of him.

This is what makes the end of a good story not just surprising but revelatory. When the end of a story feels satisfying, it's
because the conflict is resolved in a logical but unpredictable
way that reveals something about the hero's relationship to the
moral compass. An audience's sense of revelation is produced
by the realization that the story's events have demonstrated a
truth we do not yet understand but that may become evident
upon further reflection.

If this sounds difficult to achieve, try watching "What's
Opera Doc?" At the end of the cartoon, after Fudd has blasted
poor Bugs with lightning from his spear and magic helmet, he
sees Bugs Bunny's dead body and laments what he was driven
to do. Elmer Fudd repents at the end because his moral flaw has
destroyed the story goal. He has killed Brunhilda. Poor widdle
bunny. Poor widdle wabbit.

The Promise of Happiness

The language of story is about compressed meaning. Its patterns always try to point outside the story to the reality of the
audience.

The protagonist's story goal is an implied promise to the
audience that the story will resolve in a satisfying way if two
conditions are met. It will end happily (for us, anyway) as long
as the hero's conjoined selves succeed. The hero must overcome
his moral flaw *and* defeat the external forces of opposition.
Frodo must resist the temptation of the One Ring *and* toss it
into a volcano.

Now, what makes this story pattern interesting to me is not
that it's so obviously true in real life but that it obviously *isn't*.
So much of human experience contradicts the promise of life

and hope we see concentrated around the story goal. Plenty of people have gone to their deaths hoping for a happy ending. And even in less extreme cases, we see the opposite of the happy reward all the time. You do the right thing but your boss fires you anyway. You tell the truth and no one believes you. You do all the work and someone else gets the credit. That is the stuff of life. It's also why people say, "Things don't always work out in real life the way they do in stories."

The really odd thing about this contradiction is that even though situations in life don't always end happily, we still crave story goals that reward repentance and perseverance with what Hollywood used to call "the girl, the gold watch, and everything." Somehow, in spite of our own personal experiences, we see this reward pattern as *right*. It's what we want in a story.

The simple explanation for this is that people want happy endings in their stories because they aren't getting them anywhere else. Which may be true. But I think this explanation is too simple. It doesn't account for all the facts.

The most important fact it leaves out is that stories with unhappy endings are almost never successful commercially. Moreover, the ones that *are* successful commercially always have something in common: they point to the idea that the pattern itself is actually true—not escapist but prescriptive.

Put another way, stories with unhappy endings, when commercially successful, are almost always saying that the reason the hero didn't get the story goal is *because* he didn't meet the conditions. Either he didn't defeat the external forces of opposition or he didn't overcome his internal moral flaw. Either the dragon killed him or he let his hatred of wabbits destroy his love of Brunhilda.

This is why both types of stories—those with a happy ending and the far less common ones with an unhappy ending—always hold out as *right* a pattern of rewards based on overcoming internal and external conflict. Put simply, the language of story is telling us that a story will end happily if the hero (1) overcomes temptation and (2) defeats the bad guy.

Even when we don't like a particular story or that simplistic pattern, we can't help but react emotionally to its formula. We seem to unconsciously recognize and desire this kind of prescription for life—even though it doesn't seem to work. And how weird is that? Are we all really using a Darwinian flight simulator that's telling us to press the wrong buttons? Or is there another, more surprising explanation?

What if the problem isn't with the flight simulator but with the airplanes—and we've greatly misunderstood what our lives are about?

What if the moral compass is a real representation of a real protagonist but we're all wrong about the story we're meant to be living?

What if I'm not the hero of my own life?

In the next chapter we'll try to answer these questions by applying the principles of theme, context, and characterization to a surprisingly hidden Old Testament story.

8

THE FOURTH MAN

The hardest thing to live with all those years afterward was that he'd seen the atrocity coming and so had no excuse for his betrayal.

How many days had he watched from a palace window as the massive pit, dug by an army of sweating workmen, went deeper into the soil? Or listened to the pounding of nail into plank as royal scaffolds rose a cool distance from what promised to be an astonishing funeral pyre? Or clenched his teeth as load after load was carted down the earthen ramp and added to the mat of oil-soaked firewood at the bottom?

Like everyone else in the city, he'd seen the statue grow next to the pit over a period of weeks. Its surface blinded the eyes with reflected sunlight, and every evening it loomed a bit taller and more brilliant.

So it wasn't lack of preparation. If anything, he'd had too much time to consider the king's edict: bow down to the towering golden idol or be tossed into the oven. No excuses, no exceptions. Deny the real God—the God of Israel who had rescued him from death once before and rescued him again from the life of ceaseless toil endured by so many of the king's captives—or die.

Nor was the problem that he hadn't steeled himself for the flames. From the moment of the first announcement he knew what he had to do. Perhaps another son of Israel could violate the covenant this way. Life, after all, was life. But in his case there was no excuse for it. He had a responsibility to God and to the king, and now both had abandoned him. Something would have to give.

To that end he'd prepared a special appeal, a short speech born of prayer and fasting: *I am your humble servant, and I will serve you faithfully, but if that faithfulness can be purchased with fear, my lord, then it isn't worthy of you.*

He had hoped, dimly, that such an obvious truth would snap the king from madness. The king had suffered a disturbing dream, a nighttime vision of a statue with a golden head, silver shoulders, bronze belly, iron legs, and brittle clay-and-iron feet, each metal representing a future kingdom, and each kingdom less glorious than the previous one. The golden head was the king's head, his kingdom, and why suffer the fate of fools when he was the king? The great Nebuchadnezzar would change the times and boundaries set by the God of heaven by casting a new idol from a new vision—a better world by royal decree. Diplomats from every nation would swear loyalty to the gold standard, the glorious kingdom of now— embodied in a massive idol plated head-to-toe in gold—so that every kingdom would henceforth be the king's kingdom, may he live forever.

Of course it would never work. Even kings didn't live forever, and diplomats would bow to a dog if it were dressed in purple. Yet here they all were, waiting for the royal signal.

Because when the time came he had said nothing. He hadn't even *thought* of speaking. Instead, the reality of the moment had overwhelmed him.

A workman bowed to the king from the edge of the pit and tossed a flickering torch over the side. Nothing happened at first; then a small tongue of fire breached the surface, dancing from log to branch to beam, and the furnace coughed a rattling sound like teeth grinding.

Alive with sparks, a dark column of smoke curled skyward. The air tasted foul and oily as a wave of heat surged over him.

Off to his left beneath the scaffolding, musicians bleated a chorus of half-hearted tones before launching their processional. As if in answer, the king's officials and visiting dignitaries fell forward in a human ripple.

Even as he sank to his knees he saw the three young rulers, fellow Israelites and captives from Jerusalem, standing upright. Worse, they saw him.

But it was too late. Too late to stand up. Too late to offer his pathetic speech. Besides, who could have heard it above the noise of the fire and the music?

Then the music died away in a sort of strangled whimper and he could see that higher up on the platform the king stood with his hands braced on his hips. Courtiers lined up beneath him, shouting and pointing at the three rebels.

He turned his face away, wishing the moment would end, wishing he would have had the courage to remain standing as Hananiah, Mishael, and Azariah were led around a square of prone worshipers and over to the scaffold.

Then he was *glad* he hadn't tried to make his speech and grateful to be lying here in the dirt and grass instead of standing between those guards, because King Nebuchadnezzar was furious and there was no way those three young men were going to be allowed to live.

That was the worst of it, the sense of relief. Afterward he could never shake the memory of his enormous gratitude at having done the wrong thing, the betrayal that made him a traitor but also meant he could lie unseen on a little spot of earth and cling to life awhile longer.

The king was raging, his voice almost melodic with lilting fury: ". . . if you are ready to fall down and worship the image I made, very good. But if you do not, then what god will be able to save you from my hand?"

On the far side of the pit, men brought a cartload of wood and shoved it, wheels and all, over the edge. A second wave of heat radiated out, twisting the grass in front of his face. He felt as if someone had stuffed a dry rag down his throat, but he couldn't now look away.

Mishael spoke, his voice quiet at first and then louder: ". . . God will rescue us from your hand, O king. He will. But even if he does not, we will not worship your image of gold."

Whatever he'd been expecting, whatever his compatriots had been expecting, the reality of the thing was worse. Soldiers tied their hands and feet, then carried them squirming to the head of the ramp and tossed them over. A shower of sparks rose up as the writhing bodies hit the wood, a wave of embers that wrapped the soldiers above in fire and set them ablaze.

Their screams—the screams of those soldiers burning alive—would never again be far from him. But now the blasphemous gratitude was back and he realized he wasn't the man he had been, wasn't the man he had thought himself to be, though Nebuchadnezzar was wholly and entirely himself.

He hadn't thought the ninety-foot statue a good likeness, but now he saw that he'd been wrong. The king's master craftsmen had understood their master better than he, had seen the king more truly. For the king himself was but an image of the idol, a hollow wooden shell veneered in gold, unmoving and unmovable.

But what did that make him? His prepared speech came back to him and he juggled the words in his mind like hot coals: *If that faithfulness can be purchased with fear, my lord, then it isn't worthy of you.*

Isn't worthy of you.

No. He wasn't. He never would be. Those weeks of fasting and prayer had been as meaningless as his own intention, as meaningless as his faith. Where was the God of Israel now?

The king cried out and leaned over the railing of the royal platform. For the space of a breath the flames died down. "Weren't there three men thrown into the fire?" the king asked. "Why then do I see four men walking around unbound and unharmed? And the fourth looks like a god!"

Four men. There were four men in the fire. And one of them looks like a god. The God of his fathers. The God of Israel. But it should have been him.

It should have been Daniel.

The Story in the Text

This is not the story we know.

Of course I've taken liberties with many details, including the narrative voice. But I'm interested in the idea that this imaginative retelling is problematic—the problem being that we don't see the link between Nebuchadnezzar's dream of a statue and, in the very next chapter, the building of a real one. Worse, we don't see Daniel there bowing down with the other satraps when Hananiah, Mishael, and Azariah are tossed into the flames.

Daniel bowed down? Huh?

In many circles the idea seems speculative, if not downright heretical. I believe this is because we've been taught to read the Bible as an anthology, a collection of holy fables and moral precepts and puzzling aphorisms. We take a text-first approach that seeks to understand the forest of Scripture by analyzing seventeen varieties of pine needles.

I've asked many people who love and study the Bible where Daniel was when Shadrach, Meshach, and Abednego were thrown into the fiery furnace. Most answered that they hadn't considered the question. Some said they didn't know. One replied that Daniel was probably on vacation. But everyone looks at me in disbelief when I say he was bowing down to the golden statue along with the rest of the heathen hordes—that the text implies it and the story's dramatic structure depends on it.

Before I explain the latter, it's worth pausing to consider the textual hints about Daniel being present at the furnace incident even though he isn't mentioned by name:

1. Daniel was the chief administrator over the province of Babylon (2:48).
2. All the provincial rulers were summoned to the dedication (3:2).

3. All the provincial rulers *assembled* for the dedication (3:3).

4. Everyone bowed down to the statue except Shadrach, Meshach, and Abednego (3:7).

The logic of this is so simple it should be hard to miss. But we do miss it because we've been trained to ignore the implied, the subtle, and the metaphorical when we encounter it in the Scriptures. Is it possible Daniel was away on business or sick and unable to attend? Could he have been carrying out some command of the king that required his absence? Might the fact he isn't mentioned by name in this chapter be meant to imply that he isn't actually present? Yes, these are all possibilities. But they are interpretations that ignore the stubborn "all" statements of the points above. And they neutralize the dramatic structure of the story, which plays out in a recognizable *success— success—failure—success* pattern.

We've been desensitized to the scope and power of story in the Bible. Because our sermons and devotionals and commentaries specialize in dissection, we've only ever seen the thing splayed out like a frog on a cutting tray, skin peeled back, organs exposed. We rarely see what a living Bible story looks like hopping about and splashing in the water.

When we disconnect the stories of the Bible from the source of their emotive power, we blind ourselves to their significance. We should be feeling them as stories before analyzing them as doctrine. We should begin at the intersection of narrative and audience: emotion.

Neuroscientist Iain McGilchrist writes, "Feeling is not just an add-on, a flavoured coating for thought: it is at the heart of our being, and reason emanates from that central core of the emotions, in an attempt to limit and direct *them*, rather than the other way about. Feeling came, and comes, first, and reason emerged from it."[1] This isn't just a statement on the origins of mental processing. This is how stories work. It's how they're designed to work because they mirror our experience of life. And because we are wired for story, and the Bible is wired for human nature, we have the whole process backward. We have it so backward that it's almost impossible to recognize the problem without a forced paradigm shift.

It took me years to realize I needed to ask the question, *Where is Daniel when Shadrach, Meshach, and Abednego are being tossed into the furnace?* I was so used to reading the account as a self-contained lesson on God's faithfulness that I couldn't imagine it as a dramatization of human failure. It took me even longer to understand that Daniel's story arc was much deeper and richer when read as a story of redemption. What's more, this story-first approach highlighted Christ in the text in a way I'd never noticed.

Character Arcs

To understand how Daniel's arc indicates a narrative theme without stating it explicitly and thereby destroying its power of relevance, we only need to recognize its structural signposts.

The primary signpost in the story of Daniel is his character change.

All stories are about change. They are about more than this, of course, but underlying the common elements of characterization, theme, and context is the necessity that *things matter*. A story in which nothing changes isn't a story but a series of events. One might say that the most essential aspect of any story is that, in the end, things are different than they were in the beginning. And the second most essential aspect of any story is that the change we see at the end must happen *because of* what happens in the middle. Stories depict change as a result of identifiable causes.

Thus stories, like life, usually have a beginning, a middle, and an end. Unlike life, this three-part chronology is reduced to a familiar pattern that we must understand now as causal in

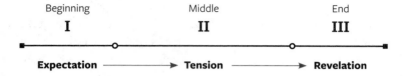

nature. That is, a story's expectation doesn't just *precede* the tension, it *causes* it; and its tension in turn causes its revelation.

The goal of this pattern isn't merely to show something happening from a distance. Stories aren't diagrams or how-to manuals. They aren't product demos. Stories are emotional journeys, and as such, they aim primarily to create emotion in the audience. All stories try to make us feel something—and not just any something but a *precise* something. The best stories create specific emotions that serve and reveal their theme. No one laughs at the end of *King Lear*. Instead, the play's feeling of deep and tragic loss undergirds its premise that we make our own torments.

The emotion one feels at the end of a great story is one of the best indicators for discovering its underlying meaning. The tears of a tragedy and the laughter of a comedy are both signposts about what the storyteller intends.

The book of Daniel is filled with these moments of change, both in the longer story arc of Daniel and in the smaller arcs of Nebuchadnezzar, Belshazzar, and Darius. Interestingly, the three young men fed to the furnace have no clear arc. They don't change, and even their moment of courage happens off-screen. That is, their agonizing decision to remain standing is not shown to us as it happens, but is only explored after it's reported to the king. The other four main characters have a story arc shaped by their individual flaws.

Nebuchadnezzar's triple arc of dream/statue/madness ends in a moment of humility based on revelation. "Everything he does is right and all his ways are just," Nebuchadnezzar says. "And those who walk in pride he is able to humble" (Dan. 4:37).

Belshazzar's arc is simpler and darker. Failing to heed either the supernatural writing on the wall or Daniel's interpretation of it, he dies in his pridefulness.

Darius the Mede, though vain enough to be baited into declaring himself godlike, at least tempers his vanity with regret. He spends a sleepless night in the palace hoping—perhaps even praying to someone other than himself—that his most trusted adviser will be delivered by the Hebrew God. When Daniel is vindicated by the same *malak* (angel) who delivered Shadrach, Meshach, and Abednego, the king orders the court schemers thrown to the lions.

Each of these character arcs is based on a decision that results in change. While these decisions aren't central to the story, they are indicators of a theme: *true power flows from humility*. The point of these arcs is that they light the path for Daniel's larger and more complex character arc.

It's easy to read the story of Daniel as a series of anecdotes about a spiritual superman. Compared to the kings of Babylon, Daniel is a great man of God, flawless in his knowledge and humble in his demeanor. For years I thought of him as the perfect prophet.

But how did Daniel get so humble? Elsewhere the story shows us that power doesn't instill meekness but pride. And Daniel walks the halls of power longer than anyone. How then does he avoid the same error that trips up the kings he serves? Why is he able to tell Belshazzar that he needs no gifts or promotion to do his job? Or, more impressive still, tell the king in front of a thousand nobles to repent of wickedness?

Daniel's Arc

The answer is found in Daniel's character arc. To have an arc, a character must begin with a flaw, something that pushes them to a moment of decision. Madeleine L'Engle explains it this way: "It is the ability to choose which makes us human. This ability, this necessity to choose, is an important element in all story. Which direction will the young man take when he comes to the crossroads? Will the girl talk with the handsome stranger? Should the child open the forbidden door?"[2]

In the six-chapter narrative that tells his story, Daniel faces four dilemmas:

1. When offered unclean food, Daniel resolves "not to defile himself with the royal food and wine" (1:8). Instead, he asks that his vegetarian diet be tested.

2. When threatened with death over Nebuchadnezzar's mysterious dream in chapter 2, Daniel asks the king for time and urges his three friends to pray for mercy. God responds by granting Daniel a vision.

3. When commanded to worship the golden statue in chapter 3—assuming he's present as one of the "all" who are summoned and assembled—he bows down.

4. When told of Darius's decree about not praying to any god except him, Daniel goes home and prays to the God of Israel—with his windows open (6:10).

These dilemmas increase in scope and severity. Each one is harder and scarier than the last. Such a pattern creates narrative tension—the driving force of a story's middle section—and the resulting pressure eventually exposes Daniel's character flaw. The author cranks the handle of a dramatic jack-in-the-box until his weakness pops out.

The first test of Daniel's character is a dilemma of pleasure/conformity. It's not a carrot-or-stick situation. It's a carrot-or-carrot-cake situation. One can imagine the thoughts going through the minds of the four friends: *Where's the harm? What choice do we really have?* Daniel's response is likewise mild but also unusually wise for a young teen: *Please test our plain diet. We'll comply if it doesn't work.*

The second dilemma is one of dependence. The king has ordered his wise men to not just interpret his dream but tell him what it was. Like an agnostic who's seen a ghost, Nebuchadnezzar is probably testing their connection to a spiritual reality he doesn't understand. Their choice is to demonstrate real spiritual power or die as impostors—die scheming or pleading for mercy or trying to escape the palace and the region and the country.

This second dilemma, though it carries horrifying consequences, isn't much of a dilemma, for none of the magi face strong but opposing desires. They all want to live; they just don't know how. "Tell me my dream and then interpret it" is a puzzle only God can unravel. And that of course is the point. Daniel and his friends are center stage for a miracle that ought to give them confidence when the king's ego explodes in the next chapter. Instead, only three people stand when the music plays.

But if Daniel's arc is built around a significant failure, shouldn't it be triggered by some internal character flaw or compromise? And wouldn't the story be signaling such a problem along the way? Here again it's possible we've missed the story's structural signposting, which repeatedly explores the tension between humility and pride.

I would suggest such a flaw *is* present in the text—and right where we might expect it. Just after Daniel's success interpreting Nebuchadnezzar's dream, the king falls prostrate before him, pays him homage or worship, and orders that an offering and incense be presented to him (2:46).

Now, we're not told how Daniel responds. There's no mention of him *accepting* this reverence, nor is there any indication he *corrects* the king as Peter did Cornelius in Acts 10:25. Hebrew scholar Robert Alter captures the ambiguity when he notes that there is no judgment present in the text, but also that "it looks suspect from a monotheistic point of view."[3]

However, the king's act of prostration is a strange detail to include here if it means nothing, because it's the very thing Shadrach, Meshach, and Abednego *refuse* to do in the next chapter.

Meanwhile, Daniel is elevated, lavished with gifts, and retained at the royal court—all types of rewards he will eventually have the humility to decline.

Daniel's Den of Lions

This is why I suggest that Daniel's story arc is one of failure and redemption. If Daniel isn't bowing down to the golden statue then he has nothing to learn and, in story terms, nothing to show us. The account of the fiery furnace isn't there to teach Shadrach, Meshach, and Abednego. It's there to teach Daniel, Nebuchadnezzar, and us.

Us most of all. Because God isn't just after changing Daniel or the three kings. He's after the transformation of the whole world. And so often the most significant changes come from failure.

Thus, the moment of Daniel's failure is highlighted by the story as a setup for his redemption. This becomes obvious when the entire narrative is viewed as a whole, with Daniel one of the "all" who bowed down in order to save himself.

Sure, we have our commentaries and sermons and anecdotal dissections. And we have the plain text of the Scripture. Yes, and of course the angel in the fire, the *malak* who appears as one of the gods to Nebuchadnezzar, was Christ himself in the flames. Of course he was. We've been told this in a dozen sermons—and an excellent point it is.

But what must have been going through Daniel's mind when he heard the king say, "Weren't there three men that we tied up and threw into the fire? . . . Look! I see four men walking around in the fire, unbound and unharmed" (3:24–25).

Four *men.*

Four.

Was he thinking that the fourth man should have been him?

Instead, Christ took his place in the fire, and for decades Daniel would have to live with that knowledge, with the memories of what he'd seen and heard and done. Worse, he'd have to live with what he'd *not* done.

If anything could make a man humble it is this. Because afterward Daniel's friends are commended by the king he has both served and, by his silence, betrayed. His friends are promoted for their courage. Yet he, Daniel, still walks the halls of power. He still outranks them, is still adviser to the king. There is no recorded rebuke from anyone, including God, and if there were it couldn't be harsher than the one he has heard from the mouth of Nebuchadnezzar: *I see four men walking around unbound and unharmed.*

Is it any wonder that when his enemies fashion a law against prayer Daniel rushes off to pray? Is it any wonder that he flings open his windows? Or goes meekly with his accusers? Or offers no defense for his so-called crime? Daniel goes to the den of lions as silent as a lamb—as silent as the lamb of God.

Of course he does. He missed the opportunity of faithfulness once; he isn't about to fail a second time. He isn't looking for a way out. Maybe he doesn't trust himself to speak. Maybe he thinks that if he opens his mouth someone will come to their senses and set him free. And he's waited so long for this chance to go back and do what he ought to have done the first time. Back then he would have faced death in the company of his friends; now he will do so alone.

But this isn't just Daniel's dilemma. It's the dilemma of every disciple of Jesus. We see Christ in the flames and so come to understand he has taken our place. But afterward there isn't the slightest rebuke from heaven. We would welcome a rebuke, but it doesn't come. It will *never* come. The fiery furnace has burned out. The guilt has faded. The fear of kings and counselors has vanished like the mist it always was. All that remains of the moment is a piercing awareness of the presence of the *malak* in the fire.

God was there, and never more there than in that moment when the flames were hottest.

Off in the distance you can almost hear his voice speaking through the crackling heat: *Whoever would come after me must take up his furnace and follow.* So Daniel, like every Jesus follower, takes up his open-air prayer and meekly follows God's *malak* to a den of not-meek lions.

Ironically, this is probably the shortest night of Daniel's life, for this is when he encounters what he's always beheld from a distance. Seen through the lens of story, this encounter is the climax of his narrative arc. Here is Daniel's dramatic change and third-act moment of revelation.

All his life, including those years in the palace serving Nebuchadnezzar, Belshazzar, and now Darius, Daniel has been a conduit for the living God, the God of Israel. He is a great man and a humble man. He is a man of knowledge and extraordinary wisdom. But his relationship to God has always been secondhand.

Oh, he knows God. That is, he knows who God is. God is "the God of my ancestors" (2:23) and "the God of heaven" (2:37, 44) and "the revealer of mysteries" (2:29). God is "the great God" (2:45) and "the Most High God" (4:24; 5:18, 21) and even "the God who holds in his hand your life and all your ways" (5:23). But it isn't until Daniel emerges from the den of lions that his language about God changes. It's here that he embraces what others have been saying all along—namely, that the living God is *his* God.

"Daniel," Darius asks the next morning at dawn, "servant of the living God, has your God, whom you serve continually, been able to rescue you from the lions?" And Daniel replies, "May the king live forever! *My* God sent his *malak!*" (6:20–22).

It's easy to miss this change of heart, this change of relationship between Daniel and his God, especially when we read Scripture looking for the presence of propositional truth rather than its presence in the form of a Person. It's also easy to miss that what happens next narratively—chronologically—when he emerges from the den of lions is found in chapter 9, which begins, "In the first year of Darius son of Xerxes" (9:1).

Mere days or weeks after Daniel steps out of his own trial of testing, his own "fourth man" moment, he embraces the paradox of sonship: he has failed his God, but God has not failed him. Now he doesn't just know about God. He knows God personally.

Chapter 9 is Daniel's prayer of repentance, written in the humility of complete surrender. He has come to terms with his own failure, a failure which mirrors that of all Israel, and discovered that God is willing, even eager, to forgive. Here in chapter 9 the eighty-year-old Daniel finally addresses God by his personal name, YHWH, the name revealed to Moses. Daniel has at last moved from knowledge of a universal Creator to intimate knowledge of a Savior. It is thus to YHWH that he addresses his prayer of forgiveness, calling on that name for the *first* time and *seven* times.

And it is to that Name—a Name with which Daniel now fully identifies—that he places his final appeal: "Lord, listen! Lord, forgive! Lord, hear and act! For your sake, my God, do not delay, because your city and your people bear your Name" (9:19).

VOICE

9

THE SENDER AND THE SIGN

Fairy tales are often distinguished by their unique voice, which is deliberately crafted to imitate the oral traditions from which such stories originate. "Once upon a time" and "happily ever after" are not just the convenient signposts of storytellers. They are portals to a certain type of narrative art that in the past two centuries has been creatively utilized by such writers as George MacDonald, J. R. R. Tolkien, and C. S. Lewis.

But we now live in an era of industrialized storytelling, and it's easy to forget that behind the narrator-audience transaction there is a third party—the one shaping the story through structure, word choice, character development, and every narrative decision down to the length and frequency of dramatic pauses. This is just as true of the film director and novelist as it is of the parent improvising a bedtime fairy tale.

Every storyteller stands behind the drawn curtain of their work. Though we can't see them, we are sometimes awakened to their presence. And occasionally the whisper of a motivating authorial presence may be heard from backstage calling the story to life.

Two Voices

In literary parlance, *voice* describes the way a story is told, the combined choices that together communicate the essential personality of the one telling the story.

A *narrative voice* helps create a story's mood and determines the sorts of things that can rightly and honestly be included in the telling. Sam Spade's noir narrative in *The Maltese Falcon*, for instance, calls to mind a unique tradition of American detective fiction—the hardboiled PI who lurks in the shadows searching for justice and love but finding only truth. The voice of Sam Spade is not the novel's *authorial* voice, which belongs to Dashiell Hammett. Instead, Spade's voice is itself a fictional creation, an imaginary personality expressing itself through the telling of the story.

Here's an illustration of the difference between the narrative and authorial voices from what many consider to be the greatest American novel, *The Adventures of Huckleberry Finn*. In the excerpt that follows, what we read is not a direct representation of the voice of Mark Twain, a.k.a. Samuel Clemens. Instead, the narrator is Huck Finn himself.

Huck's personality—Huck as the driver and protagonist of the story, indeed everything about Huck, including his voice—is an invention of the story's author. But this doesn't mean Mark Twain isn't also present. In fact, Huck's narrative voice is a filter through which Twain communicates his own perspective on the world. Some things Huck says ring true for his fictional personality but are not true about Twain's.

Twain often uses this parallelism of voice for the sake of humor, as in the following excerpt when Huck finds a sappy poem written by a deceased teenager:

This young girl kept a scrap-book when she was alive, and used to paste obituaries and accidents and cases of patient suffering in it out of the *Presbyterian Observer*, and write poetry after them out of her own head. It was very good poetry. This is what she wrote about a boy by the name of Stephen Dowling Bots that fell down a well and was drownded:

Ode to Stephen Dowling Bots, Dec'd

And did young Stephen sicken,
And did young Stephen die?
And did the sad hearts thicken,
And did the mourners cry?

No; such was not the fate of,
Young Stephen Dowling Bots;
Though sad hearts round him thickened,
'Twas not from sickness' shots.

No whooping-cough did rack his frame,
Nor measles drear with spots;
Not these impaired the sacred name,
Of Stephen Dowling Bots.

Despised love struck not with woe,
That head of curly knots;
Nor stomach troubles laid him low,
Young Stephen Dowling Bots.

O no. Then list with tearful eye,
Whilst I his fate do tell.
His soul did from this cold world fly,
By falling down a well.

They got him out and emptied him;
Alas it was too late;
His spirit was gone for to sport aloft,
In the realms of the good and great.

If Emmeline Grangerford could make poetry like that before she was fourteen, there ain't no telling what she could a done by and by.[1]

It is this last line that most clearly illustrates the point. The poem Emmeline wrote is awful—so awful it's funny. We know this, and Mark Twain knows that we know this, but Huck doesn't know this. He thinks the poem is great art, which is what makes the whole thing so much fun to read.

In a sense, this *is* great art. It is a great illustration of the art of irony and the art of storytelling. Huck remains perfectly in character as he tells the story. And behind him, perhaps chuckling himself, Samuel Clemens the author may be heard bringing this narrative to life.

Are the parallels for Scripture here too obvious to mention? Each of the books of the Bible varies in its narrative voice while remaining consistent in its authorial one. And often the purpose of one seems to be at odds with that of the other, when in fact both are working together to create a larger picture, a more complete and artistic story. Finally, when all is said and done, the controlling ethic behind these variations is the story itself. To quote Eugene Peterson, "Story is the primary way in which the revelation of God is given to us. The Holy Spirit's literary genre of choice is story."[2]

The Voice of Revelation

The Old Testament book of Ecclesiastes addresses the idea of a cosmic authorial voice. To understand its significance, we must briefly consider the relationship human stories have to ultimate meaning.

Sometimes attributed to Solomon, Ecclesiastes is filled with puzzling meditations on the nature of the world and humanity's place within it. If the "Teacher" of the book is really Solomon, then it was written by a man with plenty of time, virtually limitless resources, an incredible intellect, and wisdom imparted to him by God for the searching out of answers.

By the end of Ecclesiastes, Solomon concludes that the problem of ultimate meaning is unsolvable: "No one can comprehend what goes on under the sun. Despite all their efforts to search it out, no one can discover its meaning" (8:17). Notice he says we can't *discover* it. He doesn't say we can't *invent* it. Meaning exists, but "under the sun"—that is, within the scope of the material universe—our attempts to arrive at an ultimate meaning by ourselves will always fail. In short, such answers are beyond the reach of human reason.

This makes sense if you understand the implications of the idea that *meaning is one thing pointing to another*. The cosmos cannot be the origin of its own meaning, nor can anything within it. All of the created universe is, by definition, meaningful only in its relationship to something else, to its creator or Creator, to that which meant for each thing to have a place of significance. Put another way, if meaning cannot be derived from within, then the universe is either meaningless or it depends on something outside the circle of the material universe for its significance and reason for being.

Solomon's dismay isn't the end of the biblical narrative. But as we saw with Job, humanity had no point of reference. What we needed was for truth—a meaning derived from the outside—to break into the closed circle of the material universe.

That point of connection, or portal, between the material and the nonmaterial is called *revelation*. Revelation is not the same thing as faith, but it is the basis of faith because faith is a response to revelation. That's why faith is necessary to spiritual regeneration, for a ghost to inhabit the machine. Perhaps that's why Jesus said that everyone born of the Spirit is like the wind: you can't tell where they come from or where they're going (John 3:8). Their motivations and driving purpose are invisible; the source is outside the box of the material realm.

Semiotics, the study of signs, connections, and meaning, can be useful in wrestling with the implications of how meaning originates and is interpreted.[3] The diagram below illustrates the four basic elements of simple sign systems.

The **sender** is the person or group sending the message.

The **sign** is the delivery mechanism (e.g., physical letter, audible command, digital text message).

The **message** is what's being communicated.

And the **receiver** is the one interpreting the sign.

All this should be somewhat intuitive. When I need to cancel a class, for instance, I typically send an email to my roster of students. That situation is represented in row 1 of the diagram: the *teacher* sends an *email* announcing *no class tomorrow* to the *students*. Sender, sign, message, receiver.

Row 2 is similar: a chartered cruise is thrown off-course by a storm and shipwrecked on a deserted island. Perhaps the castaways use deadwood to spell SOS on the side of a hill. These letters, the internationally recognized code for "Save Our Souls," are a plea for help. When this sign is seen by the skipper of a Coast Guard rescue ship, the castaways are saved.

But what happens in situations where the categories are not so obvious? After all, we've been looking at ultimate meaning, at revelation as an immaterial connection between the universe and its Creator. How do situations that are easily explained in human terms—with human situations and human messages— illuminate something as complex as "the *meaning* of life"?

	SENDER	SIGN	MESSAGE	RECEIVER
1	Teacher	Email	No class tomorrow	Students
2	Castaways	SOS	We need help!	Coast Guard

The Sender and the Sign

Row 3 in the diagram below suggests an answer. When I'm the sender of the message, the process of meaning-making seems straightforward. I know what I mean to say when I email my students; if there's a breakdown in communication, I can typically figure out where it happened. Perhaps there's a typo in my email, or maybe I sent it to the wrong roster. Perhaps one or two of my students stayed out too late and didn't read the email carefully. As receivers of my message, they have less insight into what I intended, but the context and wording of my email will at least demonstrate that this four-element *process* is clear. Their professor is giving them information about the next class.

Row 3 represents Solomon's despair. When I'm neither the sender nor the receiver—when I'm the *sign*—what's the message? And who sent it?

Solomon answered the second question but not the first. In fact, he seemed to consider the second answer so obvious that he made no real attempt to prove it. In his view, the answer of ultimate origins was already there in every human heart. What wasn't there was what it all *meant*.

I have seen the burden God has laid on the human race. He has made everything beautiful in its time. He has also set eternity

	SENDER	SIGN	MESSAGE	RECEIVER
1	Teacher	Email	No class tomorrow	Students
2	Castaways	SOS	We need help!	Coast Guard
3	?	**You**	?	The world

in the human heart; yet no one can fathom what God has done from beginning to end. (Eccles. 3:10–11)

The problem with positing God as the sender, especially to those in a culture shaped around radical individualism, is that it leaves the message of our lives, the very meaning of our existence, in the hands of someone else. Since we can't have that, we sweep away any notion of dependence on God, even for meaning, and search for ultimate significance within ourselves. This at any rate is what mythologist Joseph Campbell concluded when he said, "There's no meaning. What's the meaning of the universe? What's the meaning of a flea? It's just there. That's it. And your own meaning is that you're there."[4]

Our postmodern solution is to remove the divine Sender completely. But we won't be satisfied by Solomon's honest but existentially distressing question marks. A fully self-absorbed individualist cannot accept question marks in the Sender and Message columns. Neither can we tolerate the world, large as it is, standing there in the Receiver column to receive the meaning of our lives. Is my life really about someone else, even seven billion someones? Surely it must be about something bigger still. And what could be bigger than the world of the self?

	SENDER	SIGN	MESSAGE	RECEIVER
1	Teacher	Email	No class tomorrow	Students
2	Castaways	SOS	We need help!	Coast Guard
3	?	**You**	?	The world
4	[You]	**You**	[Pick something]	[You]

Besides, the very point of placing the self in the position of sender as well as sign is that by doing so one can receive a message of one's own choosing. Thus we arrive at row 4 of the chart on the previous page, which depicts one popular myth of meaning as it currently exists in the West. If I am the sign and its sender, then its receiver must be no less significant than myself, and its message is whatever I desire. Which is shorthand for, *I shall have no other God before me.*

The Sender Is Near

The storyteller-to-audience relationship depicted in the New Testament answers the despair of Solomon with a promise we don't expect.

Even those who believe God exists tend to think of him as distant, a million miles away and seated on a throne of judgment beyond the stars. He's out there somewhere, counting the molecules or fueling the supernovas, but if he's aware of our existence at all it's only a disinterested, fact-based awareness that prioritizes recording our good and bad deeds. He may watch the unfolding of our lives, but only through a telescope, and only to keep score. Perhaps we like that idea because it makes us more comfortable with our shortcomings. By conceptualizing the standard of perfection as abstract and remote, inhuman and unknowable, we remove from ourselves the obligation of obedience to what we do know and can experience.

This sort of sterilized, atmospheric deity isn't the one depicted in Scripture. Yes, he's often described as mysterious and transcendent, so far beyond human thought and material "likeness" that no image could accurately capture his essence. But this doesn't result in a gnostic contradiction between the earthbound and the spiritual. The God of the Bible is relational. He is present in the everyday material circumstances of human life, so "with us" even in our suffering and confusion that nothing can separate us from him.

Paul captured the unique both-and quality of this transcendent presence when describing God to the people of Athens:

> From one man he made all the nations, that they should inhabit the whole earth; and he marked out their appointed times in history and the boundaries of their lands. God did this so that they would seek him and perhaps reach out for him and find him, though he is not far from any one of us. (Acts 17:26–27)

Notice the dual nature of this description: God isn't far off from anyone, and he wants to be found. But even though God is right there—just around the corner and waiting with held breath for his image-bearing children to "reach out for him"—something has gotten in the way. He is the one waiting on us, not the other way around. He is close at hand; we're the ones who loiter uninterested a million miles off.

Jesus makes this point again and again. In fact, when he sends out his disciples, the message he tells them to deliver is, in its entirety, "The kingdom of heaven has come near" (Matt. 10:7). And that nearness was to be demonstrated through healing the sick, raising the dead, cleansing the leprous, and driving out demons—all signs of the bursting out of God's goodness. Jesus's transcendent life would transcend the separation of heaven and earth. His unfelt "nearness" would become tangible "with-ness."

Times and cultures have changed, but people weren't much different during the life of Jesus than we are today. They too had a hard time believing that "the kingdom of heaven is near." This is probably one of the main reasons the Gospels are filled with stories. The best way to ensure that an audience goes beyond understanding something rationally and owns it experientially is to package it in the vault of a good story. Some will miss what's hidden inside, especially at first, but those who eventually grasp it will be changed permanently by their internal process of vault-breaking.

The Bible's stories aren't primarily conceptual; they're metaphorical. Kenneth E. Bailey goes so far as to call Jesus a "metaphorical theologian."

> A metaphor, however, is not an illustration of an idea; it is a mode of theological discourse. The metaphor does more than explain meaning, it creates meaning. *A parable is an extended metaphor* and as such is *not a delivery mechanism for an idea* but a house in which the reader/listener is invited to take up residence.[5]

In other words, in the Bible God isn't concerned primarily with the transmission of principles and concepts that can be lifted verse by verse from the page as if they were facts to be revealed on a game show. *Love is patient and kind—true or false? What is the last book of the New Testament? How many sons of Sceva were beaten by the evil spirit in Ephesus?*

Because we've gotten this point very wrong, we've missed something important about God's nature.

The Life of Christ as a Parable

If the voice of any storyteller is a revelation of their essential personality, then the personality of God may be understood—at least in part—as the causal motivation behind the choices he made in sharing his story with humanity. Just as conferring free will to his creation must have required a massive risk on his part, so too was it risky to share his personality through the story arc of Scripture. He was bound to be misunderstood. Yet even knowing that his motives would be twisted and his actions mischaracterized, he chose to play the very long game of patient love, of nearness and with-ness, that would only begin to be fully understood when he assumed human form and lived out the story in front of us.

Such a demonstration would require more than facts and formulas. It would require extended metaphors, even chains of extended metaphors that would be layered one upon another like geological strata. This is why Kenneth Bailey must use the metaphor of a house to explain the metaphorical nature of the parables. Each story Jesus told is like a house that must be lived in to be grasped. Each parable is not a one-window residence but a place of many windows, and each window has its own "true" view of the external world.

Anyone who has listened to more than a handful of sermons will recognize the truth of this. Ask ten different preachers to give a sermon on the same parable and you'll find yourself looking out of ten different windows. Some may have similar views of the mountains in the distance, but no two will be exactly alike. Remarkably, the more time and reflection each clergy member devotes to the parable, the more unique his or her sermon is likely to be.

But the strata of meaning found in Jesus's life goes much deeper than even the parables would seem to convey. Jesus didn't just *tell* parables; he *lived* them. John remarks on this at the close of his Gospel: "Jesus did many other things as well. If every one of them were written down, I suppose that even the whole world would not have room for the books that would be written" (John 21:25). Notice that Jesus didn't just *say* many other things, he *did* many other things. Every recorded incident of his life, everything he did, was rich with layered meaning, which is why for over two thousand years preachers have unpacked not just the stories he *told* but the stories he *experienced*.

Because Jesus is the true source of all meaning—the ultimate Sender and Transcender—*meaning* followed him as if in a cloud, radiating out from him and trailing behind him like a fragrant aroma even after he moved on.

It is easy to miss that his meaning-making is directly connected to the nature of his voice as the storyteller. The reason we miss the multivalent nature of Jesus's life and teaching is probably that we fail to place ourselves in a position to hear what he is really saying. Rather than sitting at his feet as disciples, we come to him as critics, perhaps even appreciative critics. Often we come as fans in search of another great moment in which the Pharisees are put in their place or our nasty neighbors are finally told off. So we bring our postmodern presuppositions of evaluation, prepared to accept the good (i.e., what we approve of and agree with) and dismiss the outdated and unrealistic (i.e., anything that makes us uncomfortable or requires a significant change of behavior).

What we *don't* do is place ourselves in a position to receive from him directly, teacher-to-student. We keep God in a faraway place behind his heavenly telescope, wreathed in the gauzy texture of hypotheses. We keep him someplace where, though he can't do us very much good, neither can he do us any real harm.

We don't learn from Jesus because we don't go to him in order to learn. We go to him, when we go to him at all, to evaluate. Though for that matter we generally *don't* go to him. Instead, we go to a *safe* Jesus, a bobblehead Jesus, a Jesus meek and mild, a hair-parted-in-the-middle-and-sporting-sandaled-feet Jesus, a Jesus of a thirty-second cross and a ten-second descent into hell, a barista Jesus who just wants to offer a friendly word of advice.

Approaching the Story as a Disciple

The same is true, perhaps to a lesser extent, with how we approach the Scriptures. We read for facts and for knowledge and sometimes for devotion, but rarely do we read for discipleship, to be ourselves transformed. Even though we suspect, quite rightly, that real transformation only ever comes as a result of hearing and responding to the voice of God.

Kenneth Bailey suggests that in order to understand Christ's metaphorical theology we must receive his parables with "authentic simplicity." He writes, "Simply stated, our task is to stand at the back of the audience around Jesus and listen to what he is saying to them. Only through that discipline can we discover what he is saying to any age, including our own."[6] In other words, we must come to him as disciples responding to his call to "follow me." We must set aside our pride and our dependence on human wisdom and our preconceptions and our traditions. Only when we do this, when we surrender the life we think we have, are we ready to receive him and receive from him.

This isn't just a matter of imaginatively placing ourselves among the crowd listening to his parables, useful as that may be. Many among the crowds who heard Jesus teach went home as spiritually impoverished as when they arrived. For instance, even after his miraculous provision in feeding five thousand people with five barley loaves and two small fish (John 6:8–12), the crowd was nonetheless offended when Jesus revealed their real motivation, that they were looking for handouts, not the "food that endures to eternal life, which the Son of Man will give you" (vv. 26–27). As soon as he described the work required to receive the "bread of God" (v. 33), they grumbled and went away.

The prerequisite for receiving *from* him is believing *in* him. There is no other path to acquiring "the words of eternal life," as Peter called them (John 6:68–69). Mere reading isn't enough, nor is it enough to listen to sermons and podcasts (though these may be helpful in their own way). Even an exhaustive book of Bible knowledge, if such a thing were to exist, couldn't light one's path to real revelation. These things may of course be used by God to train his people. But they aren't substitutes for discipleship, for sitting at the feet of Jesus to be taught directly by him in a way that illuminates the Scriptures and brings them to life. "My sheep listen to my voice," Jesus said. "I know them, and they follow me" (John 10:27). The New Testament presents us with types—with semiotic flashes of Morse code, if you will—that reveal the startling and unexpected arrival of a new covenant through which the kingdom of heaven would manifest on earth.

The crowds that followed Jesus for free burgers and fries missed the significance of almost everything he said. Oh, they thought they understood him, at least until he seemed to intentionally drive them away by declaring that they must eat his flesh and drink his blood. But it is clear that even his disciples were generally befuddled by much of what he said until they asked him privately for explanations.[7]

We too have missed the significance of what is written, and we'll continue to miss it if we aren't willing to follow this same path of discipleship, of asking Jesus privately for a revelation of what has been made public through the Scriptures. It isn't enough to stand imaginatively at the edge of the crowd when reading the Gospels. At times we must position ourselves closer still: in the house of the Pharisee who treats Jesus disgracefully; in the boat with the disciples as a storm threatens their lives; in the courtyard with Peter as the rooster crows to remind us hauntingly of our own denials; in the sandals of Thomas who wouldn't believe without seeing.

But of course it isn't seeing that produces believing. "Faith comes from hearing the message," Paul tells us, "and the message is heard through the word about Christ" (Rom. 10:17). Nor is it enough to physically hear the words being spoken. Those who have ears to hear must also internalize the message. "Consider carefully what you hear," Jesus said. "With the measure you use, it will be measured to you—and even more" (Mark 4:24). We cannot hear what we're unwilling to hear. Which means the starting point for transformation, for learning to recognize the voice of the storyteller in one's life, is recognition of one's need.

In the next chapter we'll relive a story found in the Gospel of John. To really grasp what the story is saying, it will be necessary to apply the principles of theme, context, characterization, and voice as you read. What changes as a result of the story? How is the protagonist-narrator transformed both internally and externally? Does this incident imply anything particular for your own life?

As with the story of Daniel in chapter 8, what follows is a short reimagining of a biblical event—this time in a modern context. It isn't meant to be a substitute for Scripture. Rather, it's a tool for exploration—a way to defamiliarize what we think we already know in order to see it anew. Consider it a doorway to a firsthand encounter that you previously beheld only from a distance. It's the story of a blind man who receives his sight, and if you're a true disciple of Jesus, then this is your story too.

10

THE VOICE OF THE STORYTELLER

It was going to be one of those dry summer scorchers. Even at sunrise, Sam could already feel the day coming as a line of heat across his face. God was going to shove the whole world into an oven.

Per usual, Pop and Josey had dropped him off at the corner by the filling station, but even the familiar aromas of motor fluid and donut batter fresh from the fryer seemed dampened by the rising heat. That day even the birdsong was muted and the interstate Sunday-silent.

Sam sat on the square of memory foam Mom had found for him and leaned against the concrete block wall of the station. He'd worn that spot smooth over the years. This was his place, his corner, a spot people called "ugly" because it faced the city vehicles lot instead of the old brownstone church planted catty-corner on Fifth and Main.

He preferred ugly. Pop said it added texture to the story. Patina was a good thing, maybe even a God thing. "Life sticks to you, Sam, like a soot that don't wash off. You got it all over you, and it pays, son. It pays."

So he would sit and tug heartstrings with his five-dollar smile and eyes the color of melting snow—whatever that looked like. Whenever a car dinged the tripwire bell he would turn his face to the fresh pilgrims and let his patina show: here sat a poor blind beggar, and whatever you could spare, coins or paper, it'd spend the same, and bless you for your trouble. Old Sam wouldn't harm nobody—and wasn't even old. Been broke down all his life. Just worn out now like one of those wrecks across the street. Not so far from God that the good church folk wouldn't know him, but plenty far enough they couldn't see him.

Some were Sunday morning regulars killing two birds, gas and alms, on the way home to a roast in the oven. He recognized the Kittricks by the voices of their four kids bickering in the back of the family station wagon. Some he knew by the smell of tobacco that spilled from opened doors, or the cloying sweetness of Gucci Gold that meant Widow Spengler would be going to confession.

That morning the traveling preacher arrived in a van—a big VW by the sound and smell of it: old pizza boxes and half a dozen young men singing as they tumbled out, sneakers squeaking on the warm asphalt.

"There is a fountain filled with blood—"

"Hey, Pete, check this out."

"—drawn from Immanuel's veins—"

They were coming nearer, voices fading as they caught sight of Sam.

He gave them a big "God Bless You" smile, ready to talk religion if that's what it took. Grace was the sound of paper money sliding into his wooden "Donations Whatever You Can Spare" box.

"Friend," someone said from farther back, probably the driver just coming around from the other side of the van. "You know the way to the city pool?"

Sounds of feet scuffling, making way for the new voice.

Sam pointed right, past the pumps. "Just round the corner on Main by the post office."

Someone laughed, and Sam started to get uncomfortable. He could feel the presence of somebody standing above him, then stooping down. A moment later hands grasped his face. He started to protest, but the voice said, "This won't hurt." Then something like paste was slathered over his eyelids and Sam shoved the hands away.

"What are you doing?" He was angry now. He hadn't done anything wrong. Why did some people have to be so cruel? They could see he was blind. This sort of thing wasn't funny. It hadn't been funny in grade school and it was less funny when—

"Pete," the man said. "Go with him."

Someone took his hands and hauled him to his feet. "Let's get you to the pool."

They started singing again, following along like baby ducks, laughing and shoving each other the way young men do. *"E'er since by faith I saw the stream, Thy flowing wounds supply—"*

"What?" Pete chorused.

"Redeeming love has been my theme, and shall be till I die!"

"It's gonna be okay, okay?" Pete said. "Reverend Lovejoy has a gift."

Sam went along, not sure why, one hand clutching his donations box, the other tapping his cane. The guy next to him held his elbow, and Sam wished he wouldn't but didn't want to make trouble with so many young men surrounding him.

He smelled the pool half a block away. Heard the chain-link gate creak open. Shuffled up to the edge and stopped, suddenly fearful they'd toss him in. But they were silent again. By now his face felt warm. Too warm, like something was wrong with his eyes. Of course there was. Always had been.

"You're three feet away," Pete said. "Shallow end."

Sam knelt on the hot concrete, knees protesting, and felt for the smooth tiles of the edge. He dipped one hand in the tepid water and brushed a little onto his face. His hand came away with something smooth clinging to it like oatmeal. Repeated the process with both hands as the feeling on his face increased.

The heat.

Was it heat? It was like heat, but different. Like sound but—

"There it is!" Pete said.

Sam splashed both hands in the water, scooping it up and tossing it onto his face, soaking his T-shirt and his hair and making little dribbles of water run down his back. "What did he do?" Sam shouted at nobody in particular. "What? WHAT!"

Behind him, the groupies all laughed like they'd been in on the joke and were just waiting for the punchline.

"Reverend Lovejoy has a gift," Pete said. "And he just gave it to you."

Sam leaned back, blinking, the brightness suddenly painful in a way he had never felt before. This was light. Sunlight. Sunlight on this part of the world in front of him. And this—this was water. What water looked like. What sunlight on water looked like. What a pool looked like. What the world looked like. This was what looking looked like. Had it always been this way? So much around him, this close yet beyond his knowing?

And the young men—their voices now familiar because he was skilled at capturing the timbre of a human voice even from a laugh—they weren't laughing now. Their faces were like—like what? Like eggs about to crack from the inside, maybe.

That one must be Pete. And that one with the stubble and long sideburns must be Barty, the one who fancied himself a comedian. And that one—

"Come on," Pete said, tugging Sam's elbow. "Let's go tell him."

"He's moved the van already," someone said.

"Told us to meet him at the church."

"Then we'll go to the church," Pete said.

Standing now, Sam pulled his arm away. "Think I'll just stay here awhile."

Pete shrugged. "Suit yourself."

The young men wandered off, one of them striking up a new hymn Sam barely noticed. He didn't want to go to the church, even if he couldn't admit why. But the sun was shining and the shadows it cast through the trees were mesmerizing.

Alone, he walked to the adjacent park, still tapping the ground with his cane out of habit and because he did not want to leave it behind and most of all because he needed something familiar to hold on to and to do. He moved as if in a dream, drawn to the whisper of leaves that seemed to float in the air overhead, and he sat at a picnic table and stared.

This was what trees looked like. What leaves looked like. What the sun moving between trees did to the grass. It was a kind of magic. Light and leaf, light and water. The trees had a patina of their own. The pool had a patina. Nature wasn't just natural. It was supernatural. How had he never known this? Did everyone else know this? Was this something that must be seen to be understood? Or was it one of those things that receded, like the sound of a passing train?

The noise of people moving in the church parking lot drew him out of his reverie. He must have been staring a long time. Still he did not move until the lot emptied. He didn't want a bunch of questions, a lot of people poking at him like something they found alongside the road.

When the last car had pulled away, he tap-tap-tapped down the sidewalk and across the intersection, not even bothering with the crosswalk button, then up the tilting concrete of the front steps and through the wooden arch of the front door.

Inside, light poured through the stained glass windows, and Sam saw why people liked to come to church. It certainly wasn't for the mixed aromas of candle wax and furniture polish and cheap wine.

He tiptoed through the narthex and into the chapel, the contrast between dark and light catching in his throat. Shafts of light so thick with dust you could tie a rope to them, and every color he couldn't name. What, after all, made *red* red? He would have to ask Josey. Behind the sunlight there were dark patches, beside the altar and under the frame of the door in the back and especially around the pulpit. So much darkness. So many shadows. Probably that's what made the light stand out, thinned even as it was by the colorful glass.

He walked the center aisle, tapping the carpet with his cane and brushing the backs of pews with the fingers of his left hand. How long had it been? Nine years? Ten? He hadn't taken that money, and even when the truth came out, what had it mattered? He hadn't wanted to go back, and they hadn't wanted him. Too hard for a pastor to admit he'd been wrong, and Sam was too proud to want an apology. What did he care about it now?

The basin of the baptismal font was filled, but his glimpse inside disappointed: holy water had no patina at all.

A voice called, "Sam?"

193

He didn't turn. A lifetime of attending to sounds rather than sights had trained him to lift his chin. It didn't even occur to him to look. He knew the voice wasn't that of Pastor Olson. Nor was it Pop or Josey or even Henry, the church handyman. Still, it sounded familiar.

"Sir?" Sam replied.

"Do you believe in the Son of Man, Sam?"

Standing in the semidarkness, one hand resting on the font, Sam thought this must be the question he'd been waiting all his life to hear, though never before had he been quite prepared to hear it. The darkness that had always surrounded him now had competition. This morning he wouldn't have believed he could see. Truth was, he'd not altogether believed anyone could see.

But it was a new world now. A new reality. Church, as it turned out, held more than candles and tasteless wafers and hypocrites. Somewhere out there was a Reverend Lovejoy and his traveling band of worshiping hooligans. If he could believe a blind man could see, what else might be believed?

"I'd like to," Sam said at last. "If I knew who he was."

Then he did turn, and as he did he realized he'd been clenching his eyes shut, and when he opened them the light from the open door was piercing. And standing in the midst of that light—

"You're looking at him," the man said. "Seeing him, in fact. Hearing his voice."

"Yeah," Sam said, surprised and awestruck at the same time. "I guess I do."

The Voice of the Storyteller

In the story of the blind man from John 9, visual and audial images play significant roles in highlighting what the story means. Of course, the story doesn't mean just one thing; it means many things. But instead of standing above the Scriptures to merely read and interpret them—instead of even standing behind the crowd and watching the miracle take place from a safe distance—if we place ourselves imaginatively in Sam's shoes, in the shoes of a real blind man who really lived and really encountered the incarnate Christ, we will hear and see the story as never before, and in that order. We will hear it before we see it, because it's the voice of the Shepherd we hear before we're ever led to seeing (John 10:27).

We are privileged to understand what we cannot yet see, that Jesus spits on the ground to make a little mud with his saliva. The Water of Life mixes once again with earth to make human that which isn't living, or not really living—the clay of blind flesh. He smears it on our eyes and tells us, "Go wash in the Pool of Siloam." *Siloam* means "sent."

So we go. We obey the voice of the Lord, and when we wash the mud away our sight returns, and we go home elated because we've been touched by the divine, touched by something so far beyond our wildest dreams that we didn't believe it was even possible. This sort of thing doesn't really happen, does it? It certainly doesn't happen to someone like you or me. Miracles are for the fortunate few, for the righteous, for the lucky, for the happily self-deceived. But who ever heard of opening the eyes of a man born blind? Who ever thought God would lower himself to touch human flesh? Doesn't he know us?

Then the crushing disappointment. We thought that surely our family and friends would also be elated at our good fortune, that they would rejoice with us. It's true! There is a God in Israel. He does hear the cries of the blind!

But no. We could see it on their faces. Our good fortune was their condemnation. The comfortable lies we've all told ourselves mustn't be allowed to come crumbling down. Not for the sake of one blind man. There is simply too much to lose.

We are attacked almost immediately, in spite of the fact that these hostilities are outrageous and only prove that something else is at work behind the scenes. Dragged to court—for what? Disowned by our parents—why? Because they are afraid of the chief priests, afraid of being tossed from the synagogue as outcasts.

Then investigated. Investigated? Is being miraculously healed such a terrible thing to do? It wasn't even our idea. It was *his*. (Whoever he is.) He was the one who made the mud—and remade our eyes.

Peppered by questions, we tell them this. They mock, because of course they don't understand. How could anyone understand *this*? And no matter how many times we tell the story, it doesn't seem to make any difference. They don't want to know what really happened. They're looking for some way to spin the narrative to make it less condemning to themselves. What's wrong with them, after all, that God hasn't shown up in their lives? If he is who we say, surely he would have come to them first.

So they pressure us and throw us out of the synagogue and attack our reputation and lie about what happened. We were fine before. We were never really blind. We should have minded our own beggar business.

We have done so many things wrong—felt so many things, even reacted in anger. But we have done one thing right: we followed the voice of Jesus to the Pool of Sent and washed. And now we can see, even if what we see is that our friends and family have left us to fend for ourselves, left us alone on the outside looking in.

But we aren't alone in the end. Not really. Because at some point during that low period, that confusing state of in-between, we hear his voice again. Only this time he doesn't issue a command; he asks a question.

"Do you believe in the Son of Man?"

Which is a strange thing to ask, all things considered. After all that has already happened, who are we to believe or not believe? And what does belief matter? What could it possibly change?

On the other hand, what do we have left? And so we ask, because there is really only this one question or nothing. That is the choice. "Who is he, sir? Tell me so that I may believe in him."

Later we will have to learn to look back on our past with grace, with the charity of hindsight. How could we know what Jesus looks like when we've never before seen him? Until this moment we've only heard his voice, and that only once and only a few words.

But there's no condemnation in his response. Just a statement of fact and a reminder of what came before. "You have now *seen* him; in fact, he is the one *speaking* with you."

How could we have missed that voice—the one that commanded us to wash and be clean?

And what could we say in response but "Lord, I believe"?

The New Covenant

No one who follows that voice regrets it, even though the consequences often involve counterpoised forces of spiritual antagonism. Afterward, things may seem to get worse for a while.

But watch what happens. After the blind man is disowned and lied about and thrown from the synagogue—remember, he was a beggar and now has no source of income—after all that, Jesus comes to him.

After the middle or tension section of his story, it's not just the voice of the Lord breaking through the darkness. The moment he believes, the blind man sees Jesus. As Jesus put it, "No one can see the kingdom of God unless they are born again" (John 3:3).

I am the blind man who was given his sight. So are you—unless you are still blind. Here in chapter 9 of John's Gospel there's no option to stand among the crowd and merely observe. You might, I suppose, assume the position of a Pharisee, but that only ensures that your blindness will remain (9:41).

Jesus is the voice, the personality, of God in human form. And the new covenant for which the New Testament is named is his promise to us about what God intends for every child of God who has been "born of the Spirit" (John 3:8).

In the New Testament book of Hebrews we find a reference to a prophetic promise originally made in Jeremiah 31:31–34.

> This is the covenant I will establish with the people of
>   Israel
>   after that time, declares the Lord.
> I will put my laws in their minds
>   and write them on their hearts.
> I will be their God,
>   and they will be my people.
> No longer will they teach their neighbor,
>   or say to one another, "Know the Lord,"
> because they will all know me,
>   from the least of them to the greatest.
> For I will forgive their wickedness
>   and will remember their sins no more. (Heb.
>   8:10–12)

Notice how this is structured as a four-part covenant:

1. God will place his laws in human hearts and minds.
2. He will be our God, and we will be his people.
3. We will be taught personally by God himself.
4. God will forgive and remove our sins.

The church has focused almost exclusively on the fourth part of this promise, the forgiveness of our sins, and downplayed the promise of direct, God-to-human interaction. *Why* we have done this is not difficult to understand and is easy to condone. The sheer weirdness of what's sometimes claimed as divine revelation is enough to make even the stoutest of heart recoil. Madeleine L'Engle writes,

> Throughout the ages, our religious establishments have on occasion followed Caiaphas rather than Jesus, and this is something we must be on the alert for, all of the time. But how? How to stay open? How to make sure that the voice we hear is the voice of the Lord? There are all kinds of dirty devices that get in the way.[1]

Isn't it safer to entrust the discernment of what's holy and true to a special class of clergy, to those who have been trained in theology and biblical interpretation? Aren't we better off applying a little human reason to all this? Isn't God, after all, both rational and orderly?

Everything in me wants to shout, "Yes! Yes! YES!"

The problem with this approach is that it effectively negates two of the four promises found in the text, numbers 1 and 3 above. Moreover, we've seen what happens when we entrust someone other than Christ to act as the mediator between God and humanity. Church history is littered with spiritual casualties of those who've been wounded or destroyed by a trust-me approach to the application of Scripture to individual lives. At a conference years ago, a woman told me she never read a book that wasn't first approved by her pastor. She'd off-loaded the accountability of her own conscience to someone besides the Holy Spirit.

But do I really mean that God teaches us personally? Individually? And what exactly does that look like?

Embracing the Spirit and Scripture

Before I try to answer these questions, allow me to point out that two chapters later, in Hebrews 10, God's four-part promise is compressed into two main activities. That is, the transformation

Christians experience through the influence of the Holy Spirit can be described in terms of something that's done immediately and something else that takes place throughout one's spiritual journey:

By one sacrifice he has made perfect forever those who are being made holy.
 The Holy Spirit also testifies to us about this. First he says:

"This is the covenant I will make with them
 after that time, says the Lord.
I will put my laws in their hearts,
 and I will write them on their minds."

Then he adds:

"Their sins and lawless acts
 I will remember no more." (Heb. 10:14–17)

Put another way, God has perfected the Christian forever by removing his or her sins. But we nonetheless undergo a *process* of transformation—we are "being made holy"—by God's personal one-on-one instruction.

It's important to recognize that what's being written on the heart and on the mind is God's "laws," which may be interpreted loosely as his requirements or more rigidly as the text of Scripture. We tend to fall into one of two mistakes when evaluating what this means for us personally.

On the one hand, we err by deductively co-opting verses to support an argument or an idea those verses were never intended to make. "It's the anointing that breaks the heavy yoke" doesn't mean what some have implied by frequently referencing that biblical imagery.

On the other hand, Scripture itself, without the interpretive activity of the Holy Spirit, can be misunderstood and even twisted into a weapon. Satan can quote Scripture (Matt. 4:6). And Jesus points out that even the most learned can study the Bible for a lifetime and still miss the point: "You study the Scriptures diligently because you think that in them you have eternal life. These are the very Scriptures that testify about me, yet you refuse to come to me to have life" (John 5:39–40).

The simple solution to these two errors is to embrace both Scripture and Spirit. It's Scripture that is being written on the heart and on the mind, and it's the Spirit who is doing the writing. We are made holy, transformed into Christ's image, by a revelation of God's Word conveyed to us personally and individually by the activity of the Holy Spirit. The Teacher promised by Jesus at the Last Supper will lead us into all truth; he will bring glory to Jesus by taking from what is his and making it known to us (John 16:13–14).

To be clear, nothing about this suggests that God cannot speak to us outside of his Word nor that everything claimed as "thus saith the Lord" is actually from God. The stark and somewhat terrifying reality of the new covenant is that God has promised to teach us personally through Scripture, and also that we live in a world in which this process can easily go wrong a million different ways. And ultimately, the only safeguards we have against getting off track are (1) Scripture itself, which is the standard by which every "thus saith" must be measured, and (2) the patient activity of the Holy Spirit.

In other words, even though a lot can go wrong when we trust God to speak to us through and about Scripture, he seems to think the payoff is worth the risk.

The real question is, Do *we*?

After Emmaus

Evidence of how deeply God is committed to this process can be found throughout the Bible, but especially in the New Testament.

Space doesn't permit a deeper exploration of how prevalent this theme is, but one clear example should help to highlight the role the storyteller's voice plays in the unfolding story of Scripture.

After his resurrection, the risen Christ walks with two disciples on the road to Emmaus. This story, found in Luke 24, dramatizes the new covenant promise of God writing his law on human hearts and minds. As it does, it also compares the revelation of his Word to the healing of physical blindness.

> And beginning with Moses and all the Prophets, he explained to them what was said in all the Scriptures concerning himself. . . . When he was at the table with them, he took bread, gave thanks, broke it and began to give it to them. Then their eyes were opened and they recognized him, and he disappeared from their sight. They asked each other, "Were not our hearts burning within us while he talked with us on the road and opened the Scriptures to us?" (vv. 27, 30–32)

Christ explains what is written in the Scriptures. He doesn't tell them the future of Roman politics or describe church hierarchies. He doesn't advise them about which stock to buy or hint at who will win the World Series. Jesus opens the Scriptures. He explains what is written, and when they see him offering them bread—a semiotic symbol of God's Word—their eyes are opened too. Afterward they realize that the voice of the Lord has touched their hearts with fire.

But even though he is relentlessly committed to the promise of the new covenant, God will nevertheless allow us to miss it. Just as Jesus didn't force the crowds to understand his parables, and just as he didn't explain his stories even to his disciples until they asked him to, neither does he open our minds to the Scriptures today unless we respond to his invitation.

The blind man had to obey, had to go wash in the Pool of Siloam, in order to receive his sight. His obedience was not forced. But he *did* receive his sight. And when he was at his lowest, he saw God face-to-face.

So too does God speak into our blindness, and we can either go and wash or we can try to wipe the mud away with our hands. The choice is ours.

God's voice is foundational to his relationship with humanity. God *wants* to speak to us, but we have distanced ourselves from him and stuck our fingers in our ears. While we wait for tradition and reason and YouTube personalities to explain the difficult passages of the Bible, Jesus waits for us. He stands at the door and knocks.

He *could* kick the door in, but he won't. That isn't his style. His style is to let the ideals of the story and the free choices of individuals play out.

God is telling an incredible story. And he wants to involve us—to infuse our lives with layers of meaning we can't even imagine without him. He wants to open our eyes.

But first, those who have ears to hear must hear.

PLOT

11

RESOLVING THE IMPOSSIBLE

And so we come, perhaps surprisingly, to the resolution of the biblical story, which finds its place in the element of plot.

As a young man I had the good fortune to study creative writing with science fiction legend James Gunn, who said there are three and only three plots that form the basis of every story:

1. "Boy Meets Girl"
2. "The Man Who Learned Better"
3. "The Little Tailor"

It took me years to wrap my mind around the significance of this simple paradigm. Only when I realized that these plot types are defined by their resolution, not by any series of particular events within them, did I understand Gunn's rationale.[1] There is no limit to identifying plot types by what happens, but these are the three ways a story might end.

A story, in other words, is best understood by what type of goal it strives toward. This is why every successful novel and movie opens with clear implications about what sort of story the audience should expect. A horror movie will have a certain look from the opening frame, and that look will have little in common with a rom-com. A cozy mystery novel will not begin like a comedic fantasy. The audience needs to know what they're in for. Thus Hemingway opens *The Old Man and the Sea* with this remarkable sentence:

> He was an old man who fished alone in a skiff in the Gulf Stream and he had gone eighty-four days now without taking a fish.[2]

In the very first sentence of the novel we are introduced to the central character (an old man), the story goal (to catch a fish), a reason to care (eighty-four days), and the genre (fishing adventure).

How will this story end? I won't spoil it for you, but it's safe to assume that it involves catching a fish. Otherwise, why not start the book on day eighty-seven, or whenever the old man's unlucky streak ends?

More to the point, which plot is Hemingway using?

It isn't "Boy Meets Girl." Nor is this a "Man Who Learned Better" story. Therefore, if Gunn is right, this must be a variation of "The Little Tailor." If you've never read that fairy tale, the important thing to understand is that the story involves a humble protagonist who overcomes a series of increasingly difficult obstacles in order to win the hand of a princess (the story goal). This story type is also called the *monomyth* or the *heroic quest*, and it has been used for stories as varied as *The Labors of Hercules*, *Star Wars*, and *The Lord of the Rings*.

Each of the three plot types works because of something that happens during its resolution. That is, each sort of resolution creates an emotional reaction, a feeling of satisfaction about the world being set right.

In a "Boy Meets Girl" story, this feeling of satisfaction is created by a shift in the relational status of the central character.

Janet begins the story alone but by the end has met her perfect relational match. The tension of her need, which drives the major plot twists and reversals, is resolved only when her longing for wholeness is met, when Janet changes states from alone to together. The "Boy Meets Girl" plot is therefore about a character achieving a state of completion.

The "Man Who Learned Better" story focuses on the tension of an unresolved character flaw, sometimes portrayed as a lie the protagonist accepts as true. Ebenezer Scrooge, for instance, has traded his love of humanity for the love of money. Dickens corrects this flaw by sending four spirits into Scrooge's life to show him that his choices are destroying his own happiness and purpose. What makes this plot type effective is the emotion produced by a protagonist's dramatic but relatable change of heart.

The plot type of "The Little Tailor" or heroic quest resolves when the protagonist finally achieves the story goal by overcoming a series of increasingly difficult obstacles. In his classic work on narrative mythology, Joseph Campbell describes the pattern quite simply: "He must survive a succession of trials. This is a favorite phase of the myth-adventure. It has produced a world literature of miraculous tests and ordeals."[3]

Along the way, the hero typically lets go of a comfortable but false identity and assumes a truer but more difficult one. This act of surrender is usually linked to an act of self-sacrifice that results in the survival of their community. Luke Skywalker must surrender his dream of becoming a pilot in order to take the harder but more honest path of the Jedi. It is his final act of surrender—"Use the Force, Luke!"—that enables him to destroy the Death Star and save untold billions.

Plots of Life

What makes these three plots effective as story patterns is the emotion they create in their resolution. Life, in other words, is a story, and the story of every person's life tends to be most dramatic, most emotive, in those experiences that look like the end of a "Boy Meets Girl," "Little Tailor," or "Man Who Learned Better" story. Furthermore, each of these dramatic arcs is experienced by nearly everyone by the time they reach adulthood.

Most of us can relate to the "Boy Meets Girl" plot type, for instance, because we too have lived through the dramatic tension of unrequited love, painful miscommunication, relational wrong turns, and the heartbreak of rejection. "She loves me, she loves me not" is relatable and agonizing, which is what makes it a wellspring of dramatic power.

Similarly, the "Man Who Learned Better" plot type draws from our shared sense of moral failure—and the awful recognition of that failure when we are confronted with its consequences. This sort of story has broad dramatic power because nearly everyone has a skeleton or two in their closet. So stories that center on an act of repentance typically work by showing us the nature of our own failure as the result of accepting a seemingly innocuous lie: *No one will notice. I deserve this more than they do. It's all in good fun, right?* George Bailey believes a lie about what makes life wonderful, and only at the end of the film does he recognize the quiet life he has despised is really the most wonderful sort possible.

It doesn't take a lifetime of bad choices to create significant failures. Most of us can recall at least one humiliating act of selfishness from our teen years. If only we could have learned better before storing up those bitter memories! Which is why the "Man Who Learned Better" plot resonates across history. We all, like George, have gone astray, each of us turning to our own cringey way.

Finally, the heroic quest may be the most unexpectedly resonant of the three. Because few of us live the sorts of adventures found in monomyth stories—let alone the fantastical extremes of Jedi training or epic battles with a dragon—it is easy to dismiss such stories as wholly unreal. But this is a mistake. It isn't the fantastic or extreme elements that produce a sense of satisfaction at the end of a heroic quest. It's a sense of shared experience. These stories resolve through an achievement that comes at the cost of enormous pain and self-sacrifice. They mirror the universal human quest for identity as we journey from child to adult.

At some point every child understands that he or she is entering the community of grown-ups and so wonders what his or her place will be within it. Before long we must all face the question, *Who will I be then?*

Stories, particularly those patterned after the heroic quest, are humanity's attempt to meaningfully answer our search for identity. The monomyth pattern suggests that in becoming a new and truer version of yourself, a contributing adult, you must let go of the comfortable, selfish delusions of childhood. The heroic figure, the one admired and esteemed by the community, is the one who sacrifices for the good of others, accepting the challenges and hardships of life even to the point of death. This, at any rate, is the story we internalize. And because we internalize it, we're easily drawn to the emotions of its resolution. When Frodo stands with the ring at Mount Doom, or when Luke Skywalker fires the last shot at the Death Star, or when Indiana Jones closes his eyes at the opening of the Ark of the Covenant, we recognize the moment as universal and human. It's a relatable transformation into a new and greater identity, but one that comes with intense suffering.

In short, each of these three plot types is a dramatization of universal human experience. We long for relationship. We find peace through repentance and moral growth. We discover meaning through individual sacrifice for a larger community or public good.

Jack-in-the-Box

When I was a little boy I used to go over to the neighbor's house to play. He had a tin jack-in-the-box that played "All Around the Mulberry Bush" when you turned the handle. Eventually the lid would open and a horrifying monkey-clown would pop out.

To this day I hate those things. But that didn't stop me from cranking the handle over and over again. Sure, you're a little scared. But you shove the monkey back in, start turning, and the song begins again. And as it does, you start to feel the tension. At least when you're four.

In a sense, all stories have a jack-in-the-box structure. Their three-part chronological structure mirrors the triune human emotions that characterize a great story.

The beginning is a matter of cranking the handle in expectation. The middle reflects the tension created by the thing we know is coming. And the end is the sudden appearance of a monkey-clown.

The opening *expectation* can be as short as a single sentence or can take up many pages. Usually the expectation of the opening ends no later than 25 percent of the way into a story. This is where the first act of a screenplay usually ends, at about twenty-five minutes into a film.

The *tension* section is where our expectations are opposed by some force of antagonism or conflict that's repeatedly expressed through disasters and dilemmas. Dramatically, a *disaster* is anything that moves the plot of a story by shifting the values of a scene through something going terribly wrong with the protagonist's attempt to achieve the story goal. A *dilemma*

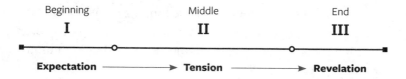

212

is a dramatic shift based on a character being forced to make a decision between two terrible alternatives.

Such opposition heightens our emotional investment in the story. In the first part we were given something to want, but in this part what we want is refused, usually in a way that creates angst about a belief we hold to be true. For example, "love always prevails" or "honesty is better than lying" or even "power corrupts." Of course, that sort of belief can't be stated overtly or the story won't work as a story. But the underlying belief will still be there. And here in the middle of the story it will be challenged and made to look weak and foolish.

The tension section of the story is where doubt comes in about something meaningful to the audience. And it comes in because what we want, which itself represents something deeper and more significant, seems to be rebuffed by something more powerful but also less right.

As the story progresses that doubt will increase, which in turn will increase our sense of tension until we arrive at the end of the story—what can be called the surprise or *revelation* moment. Robert McKee explains, "The Climax of the last act is your great imaginative leap. Without it, you have no story. Until you have it, your characters wait like suffering patients waiting for a cure."[4]

This is the moment when the monkey-clown bursts out of the box. What makes it work is that it is both predictable and unexpected. We in the audience should have seen it coming, but we didn't. The tension has been getting stronger and stronger until there seems to be no way the good guy can win, no way the truth we believe can be validated. But suddenly the unexpected happens, and we see the whole story and the whole argument in a new light. It comes as a kind of revelation. Luke Skywalker uses the Force to fire his last shot at the Death Star. Ebenezer Scrooge sees himself in the grave. The Martians in *The War of the Worlds* defeat humankind but haven't planned to defend themselves against earth's bacteria.

Surprise! The thing we hold to be true really *is* true, but not the way we expected. That's a revelation and something we feel we learned. But we didn't just learn it. We *earned* it because we went through the tension section and faced all the reasons why what we want might not be true after all. We shared in the suffering of the hero, and that suffering has affected us the way it might have if we had experienced the action of the story firsthand.

This sort of resolution produces a feeling of catharsis, and our brains get really happy. If the story is done well and we are completely transported, we'll have a rush of emotion that seems to validate the original belief. Todd Hall points out, "When people's worldview beliefs are shaken up, the resulting meaning-making can allow people to rebuild their assumptions about themselves and the world, facilitating growth. In fact, several studies have reported that the greater the threat, the greater the reported growth."[5]

Isn't that cool?

And all the while, we won't realize that the process of living vicariously through that story has actually changed us. Its suffering and resolution have convinced us of something.

And we don't even know it.

The Arc of Scripture

Understanding the dramatic arc of Scripture is essential in recognizing the mission of Jesus and what happened on the cross. We miss the significance of the Bible's dramatic structure when we don't see the story in its proper context, when we treat the life of Jesus as if it happened in a spiritual and cultural vacuum.

But dramatic whitewashing isn't our only obstacle to reading the story as a story. In separating the entire arc of the Bible into smaller stories and verses that function as mere anecdotes or sermon illustrations, we've disconnected the act of resolution from the conflict it's meant to resolve. We haven't understood that the story of Jesus is the re-creation and fulfillment of the story of Israel—a story that would resolve with every nation on earth being blessed through Abraham's offspring, the Messiah (Gen. 12:3). Our doctrine-first approach has lifted Jesus out of history and reimagined him solely as a mechanism for salvation.

But before we can understand the conflict of the Bible, we need to deal with three paradigms that have hidden the story from us.

Paradigm 1: We've Erased the Villain

We tend to read the Bible as a two-party narrative arc that pits fallen humanity against a redemptive Creator. While this is certainly one aspect of the story, it's a crippling oversimplification. Instead of the plot unfolding as interconnected disasters and dilemmas that involve all of creation, including the fallen angels, it reduces biblical history to a series of disconnected individual dilemmas: *Have you made a decision for Christ?*

The main conflict of the Bible is a clash between the kingdom of God and the kingdom of Satan. It's not a *man-versus-man* story but a *God-versus-god* story. Jesus didn't come merely to deliver humans from sin (as important as that is). Jesus came to redeem *all* creation, to take back the devil's usurped authority over the earth. Theologian Greg Boyd writes,

> Though the motif of spiritual warfare is rarely given its full due, the biblical narrative could in fact be accurately described as a story of God's ongoing conflict with and ultimate victory over cosmic and human agents who oppose him and who threaten his creation.[6]

Modern and postmodern theologians have tried to make the Bible more progressive, more rational, by explaining away its miracles and its spirit beings. They've said that miracles were the result of mass hypnosis, demons were just misunderstood psychological afflictions, and the virgin birth was lifted from mythology. First-century Christians meant well, but they were too primitive to understand that when Jesus was being tempted by Satan in the desert, he was probably hallucinating after not eating for forty days. And anyway, the conversation he had with the tempter isn't meant to be taken literally but instead shows us we must say no to bad things and yes to good things. And isn't that a nice lesson for the Messiah to have left us?

This sort of reading requires the dynamite and sledgehammers of higher critical theory, deconstruction, and what C. S. Lewis called "chronological snobbery."[7] Perhaps the most astonishing thing about these theories is that anyone still accepts them.

The Bible doesn't work as a story if the villain is removed, just as *The Lord of the Rings* wouldn't be an interesting story without Sauron and *Robin Hood* wouldn't work without the Sheriff of Nottingham. Yet we continue to misread and misplot the Scriptures because we've accepted the claims of materialists that their reality is *the* reality, that the universe is a sterile place of energy and matter and nothing else, and only an idiot would talk about the devil being real. For five hundred years the Protestant church has been telling itself that belief in a spiritual tempter was just plain medieval.[8] *And can we really bring ourselves to believe that?*

Paradigm 2: We Live in the Aftermath

The second reason we're blinded to the main story arc of Scripture is that we've viewed it from the privileged position of the aftermath of the cross. We take for granted the way the story unfolds; in fact, we are so used to the happy ending of the resurrection that even on Good Friday we fail to recognize the heavy holiness of what it represents. We don't consider the cross without the resurrection.[9] Consequently, we don't appreciate the story's resolution, what J. R. R. Tolkien described in his essay "On Fairy-Stories" as the "eucatastrophe" of history.[10]

The lostness of the world before Christ was exponentially more terrible than we've imagined it to be. We haven't wrestled with the depth of our problem, the utter brokenness of everything before the Messiah came to deliver us. Humanity was bereft of hope and doomed to a hellish existence of unceasing torment and demonic servitude.

Understanding this situation—the inexorable bondage into which humans were born, lived, and died—is crucial to the story. From the garden to the cross, Satan *dominated* the earth. Every kingdom belonged to him. He even claimed Israel, and in the wilderness he boasted to Jesus about his ownership of God's chosen people.

Note that the temptation here appears to surrender the very story goal of heaven into Christ's hands: *Is this not what you have come for?*

> The devil led him up to a high place and showed him in an instant all the kingdoms of the world. And he said to him, "I will give you all their authority and splendor; it has been given to me, and I can give it to anyone I want to. If you worship me, it will all be yours." (Luke 4:5–7)

We cannot reasonably interpret this as a lie. For one thing, it's doubtful that Satan would believe he could deceive God. Moreover, if it were a lie, it wouldn't have been a temptation.

But we need more than a rational understanding of what it meant for all humanity to be held in the irresistible grip of satanic power. We need to feel the helplessness and despair of that reality. This is what the apostle John expresses in the book of Revelation when he describes his reaction to the book's central image:

> Then I saw in the right hand of him who sat on the throne a scroll with writing on both sides and sealed with seven seals. And I saw a mighty angel proclaiming in a loud voice, "Who is

217

worthy to break the seals and open the scroll?" But no one in heaven or on earth or under the earth could open the scroll or even look inside it. I wept and wept because no one was found who was worthy to open the scroll or look inside. (5:1–4)

Some scholars interpret this scroll in the hand of God as either the Book of Life or a list of the coming apocalyptic plagues, but from a dramatic standpoint it's better seen as the title deed to earth (Jer. 32:6–12). The scroll is sealed by seven seals, probably the seven spirits of God, which is a symbolic way of indicating that the authority behind the deed to earth is confirmed by God himself. Earth's dominion derives from him, which is what makes Satan's position so strong. Adam and Eve handed over their authority, and now there is no one capable of taking it back.

Even God cannot just take it back by force, for as we saw with Job, this would be God disowning himself. If he were to take the world back through force, he would be opposing his previous judgment—a contradiction that would make the satanic lie ("You only rule by power") resonate through eternity. Instead, God operates by a sense of "fair play."[11]

No, the cosmic resolution of God's story won't come as a matter of brute power but as a matter of *worthiness*. John has seen, at the end of Revelation 4, that the Lord God Almighty is worshiped by the living creatures around the throne as *worthy*. Why? Because, in their words, "You created all things, and by your will they were created and have their being" (v. 11).

Creation shouts the worthiness of the Creator! But this isn't the question faced by humanity. The question that lies at the center of the gospel is, "Who is worthy to break the seals and open the scroll?" (5:2). Who is worthy to reign over the earth? Whose dominion is worthy—that of power or of principle? If principle, then who will save humanity from the dominion of the satanic realm?

John saw that "no one in heaven or on earth or under the earth could open the scroll or even look inside it" (5:3). This is what prompted him to weep and weep. No human ruler, no angelic guardian, no Marvel superhero would be coming to save us. God's good earth and all his human image bearers would, for all eternity, be cut off from his life and redemption and rulership.

> Then one of the elders said to me, "Do not weep! See, the Lion of the tribe of Judah, the Root of David, has triumphed. He is able to open the scroll and its seven seals." (5:5)

Into this space of soul-crushing despair the hero of the biblical story arrives. The Lion of Judah has come! The power of all powers, the Mighty One of old, the perfect and flawless Creator will do what cannot be done. He will take back the title deed of earth using not force, not violence, not supernatural wrath, but innocence. "Thus, at the cross, we are shown what it looks like for 'power-as-control' to be replaced by 'power-as-compassion.'"[12]

This is the eucatastrophe of heaven!

And it's demonstrated in a profound and shocking reversal of images that perfectly captures the reality of the crucifixion. For no sooner is the Lion of Judah announced than he appears:

> Then I saw a Lamb, looking as if it had been slain, standing at the center of the throne, encircled by the four living creatures and the elders. (5:6)

All creation expected deliverance through the power of the Lion, through his divine claws and fangs. Instead, he appeared as a helpless and humble Lamb.

A Lamb born to be slaughtered.

A Lamb about whom a new song is sung, a song of worthiness based not in creation but redemption.

219

> You are worthy to take the scroll
>> and to open its seals,
> because you were slain,
>> and with your blood you purchased for God
>> persons from every tribe and language and people
>>> and nation. (5:9–10)

That we don't appreciate the startling significance of this reversal of images shows we haven't appreciated the enormity of our doom.

Paradigm 3: We've Unraveled the Plot

The third reason we miss the main storyline of the Bible is that we've bifurcated what should be an integrated arc of two twining threads into separate and seemingly unrelated plots: the *incarnation* and the *atonement*.

The Eastern Church places at the center of its theology the incarnation of Christ. This emphasis highlights the importance of community and is reinforced by the dominance of Easter rather than Christmas as its primary holiday. That a theology focused on the incarnation would make the atonement its biggest celebration is not a contradiction. Holidays are when we take a break from that which usually occupies us. They are when, for just a few days, we do something different.

But even while this emphasis is driving home the mystery of "God with us," of the *Logos* connecting heaven and earth in a flesh-and-bone body that's simultaneously human and divine, it's dismissing as secondary the *telos*, the fulfillment or endpoint, of that duality. The bifurcated East understands better than the West that "God so loved the *world* that he gave his one and only Son" (John 3:16). What they tend to miss is the second half of that verse and its significance to the individual: "that *whoever* believes in him shall not perish but have eternal life."

This isn't to say that the Eastern Church has somehow missed the gospel message. But the gospel cannot be unraveled into two separate threads without the story being lost in the process, which is why Protestants are almost always just as biblically unstoried.

The Western church centers its theology around the atonement, the death and resurrection of Christ as the substitutionary sacrifice for our sins. Western Christians have concentrated so hard on this plot that many pastors see "justification by faith" as a complete description of the gospel message. Theologian Scot McKnight unpacks this when he writes, "A salvation culture does not require The Members or The Decided to become The Discipled for salvation. Why not? Because its gospel is a gospel shaped entirely with the 'in and out' issue of salvation. Because it's about making a decision."[13]

This is why the major celebration in the West is not Easter but Christmas. We take our vacations and spend our money and eat our biggest family meals in the winter, not in the spring. We spend weeks replaying songs like "Silent Night" and "O Little Town of Bethlehem" but have no comparable traditions around Easter. Head-to-head, Santa obliterates the egg-laying Easter bunny. And why? Because Christmas is our break from the norm. For most of the year we're consumed by a crucifixion-first theology.

While this is helpful in highlighting our need to be born again in order to see the kingdom of heaven, it misses the worldwide scope of the main storyline. Evangelicals in particular have placed so much emphasis on "decisions for Christ" that we've missed what this sort of reductionism ultimately creates: we've made many converts but very few disciples. Our half of the bifurcated story allows us to see that "whoever believes in him shall not perish" but hides from us the starting point that "God so loved the world." We miss that Jesus didn't just die for us individually; he was sent to us collectively.

This disconnection of the atonement from the incarnation lies at the root of our inability to see the conflict and resolution of the gospel, which is the good news that Jesus has fulfilled the story of Israel[14] and ushered in a new way of being. Indeed, *incarnation* and *atonement* might be understood dramatically as the *conflict* and *resolution* of Scripture. And just as a story doesn't work if its main conflict doesn't resolve, neither can a resolution be fulfilling without a conflict. Put another way, without the atonement, the incarnation stands unresolved; and likewise, the atonement is no resolution at all without the incarnation.

But how then does the incarnation of Christ introduce (or, more accurately, *heighten*) the central conflict of the Bible? And how does the atonement resolve that conflict if the conflict is worldwide rather than fragmented, prism-like, into any one individual's culpability for sin?

Opening the Seals

The answer to these questions lies in the plot of the Bible, which may be seen in a compressed form in the story of the life of Jesus. Yes, the Old Testament is more than just a prophetic shadow of the Messiah's incarnate through line.[15] Still, it *is* a prophetic shadow, and because of this the whole dramatic arc of the Bible may be seen in the interlinking narratives of Matthew, Mark, Luke, and John. Jesus didn't just defeat the power of sin; he also defeated Satan and in doing so reclaimed the title deed to earth.

This is what's happening in John's symbolic retelling of the gospel in Revelation 4–11. God's worthiness to rule is initially heralded in the angelic realm (a mirror of Job 38:7, where "the morning stars sang together and all the sons of God shouted for joy"). But that worthiness is called into question as the scroll of earthly dominion is held out. No one is worthy to reclaim earth from satanic rule. No one has the witness of God himself, God's seven spirits attesting via seven seals to the worthiness of the one who is fit to receive all honor and glory and power.

Not, that is, until the Lamb comes and, with increasing narrative tension, begins to open the seals one by one.

I don't know what sort of sound such seals would make. Perhaps it's only the whisper of wax lifting from parchment. Nevertheless, the story is told with such gravity that we might imagine each seal as resounding throughout heaven, unclasping with the audible *snap!* of a nuclear briefcase.

John thereby reveals with dramatic intensity the transfer of rulership as, seal by seal, Christ's messianic reign draws ever closer.

Snap!—The Spirit of Wisdom attests to the worthiness of Christ, and a crowned rider on a white horse rides out for conquest (6:1–2).

Snap!—The Spirit of the Lord attests to the worthiness of Christ, and on earth the result is worldwide war (6:3–4).

Snap!—The Spirit of Understanding attests to the worthiness of Christ to rule on earth, and economic chaos consumes the nations (6:5–6).

Snap!—The Spirit of Counsel attests to the worthiness of Christ, and the realm of fallen spirits begins to vomit up famines and plagues (6:7–8).

Snap!—The Spirit of Power attests to the worthiness of Christ, and the spirits of the martyrs cry out in anticipation from beneath the altar (6:9–11). *The moment is so close!*

Snap!—The Spirit of Knowledge attests to the worthiness of Christ, and the heavens themselves are shattered, the sky rolls back "like a scroll" (perhaps revealing the true nature of cosmic reality), and on earth the servants of God are set apart from the wicked (6:12–17).

Snap!—The Spirit of the Fear of the Lord attests to the worthiness of Christ, and all heaven seems to hold its breath. In fact, John tells us that "there was silence in heaven for about half an hour" (8:1).

But after this silence, heaven's sevens are reversed in dramatic parallelism. Seven angels are given seven trumpets, releasing seven plagues in succession—including three woes released at the fifth trumpet blast and four riders at the sixth—until an angel, standing on the sea and on the land, declares, "There will be no more delay!" (10:6), and the seventh trumpet announces the transfer of the dominion of earth to the reign of King Jesus:

> The kingdom of the world has become
> the kingdom of our Lord and of his Messiah,
> and he will reign for ever and ever. (11:15)

This is the plot of the gospel as viewed from the perspective of the story goal, from the end of the timeline. But it's an end we have yet to see realized. We're still in the chiastic counterpart to the aftermath of the fall, awaiting the redemption of all things even as Christ waits for his enemies to be made his footstool (Ps. 110:1; Heb. 10:13).

The Weakness of Power

The value of recognizing the transfer of dominion as the beginning of the fulfillment of the story goal of Scripture is that it reshapes our understanding of the gospel narrative. When read only as a personal salvation device, the story of Jesus raises questions that are so odd to modern readers that we scarcely know what to do with them.

Why, for instance, do demons continually try to announce the true identity of Jesus as the Holy One of God? And perhaps more baffling, why does Jesus tell them to shut up? For that matter, why does he tell those he's healed to keep the miracle a secret? And why does he tell his disciples that he was sent only to the lost sheep of Israel? Or again, if he was sent only to Israel, why does he travel to the borders of Israel and cast out demons in the nations beyond? Perhaps most baffling of all, why does he pick Judas Iscariot to be a disciple when he knows Judas will betray him?

The answers become apparent when we understand the life of Jesus as the story of the redemption of earth, the conquest of satanic dominion through an unexpected mechanism. We see this in the book of Hebrews:

> Since the children have flesh and blood, he too shared in their humanity so that by his death he might break the power of him who holds the power of death—that is, the devil—and free those who all their lives were held in slavery by their fear of death. (2:14–15)

Jesus would prevail by challenging Satan to express his strongest argument, his right to rule, in its most powerful terms. And that expression would be Satan's undoing. Paul tells us, "And having disarmed the powers and authorities, he [Jesus] made a public spectacle of them, triumphing over them by the cross" (Col. 2:15).

Fittingly, Gustaf Aulén calls this sort of interpretation of the gospel the *dramatic* interpretation. It has also been called the *classic* interpretation because it was the primary mode of interpretation for the first thousand years of church history. Today it is more popularly known as *Christus Victor*.

To be clear, I'm not attempting to fully represent that model here. Not only is *Christus Victor* an incomplete understanding of the atonement, it was never fully systematized (perhaps for good reason) by the early church.[16] Scholars have also pointed out that in some of its forms it seems to ignore the sacrificial importance of the cross.

Nevertheless, it's useful to acknowledge that the early church conceived of the gospel as a story. That story is the story of Jesus as the fulfillment of the story of Israel, and in order to understand its dramatic nature, it must be interpreted with a story lens.

The Five Elements in Scripture

Having covered the basic elements of the language of story, we're now in a better position to see the narrative conflict woven through the life of Jesus in the four Gospels. So far we've learned not just how story communicates its view of life and reality and human nature but how its basic grammar undergirds the arc of the Bible:

The setup of *theme*: This world was meant to be culti-vated by human image bearers, but our divine authority was usurped by dark, demonic powers.

The problem in *context*: The satanic lie flung at God—namely, that he only rules by power—will be refuted by a perfect human who overcomes raw power with naked principle.

The hero as a *character*: The story will only be resolved if humanity's true hero overcomes temptation and defeats the external force of antagonism, the demonic beings who inhabit the parallel realm of the spirit world.

The promise of the storyteller's *voice*: While we're not the hero of our own life story, each of us has a part to play as we follow the call of Jesus. God promises to teach us one-on-one by his Spirit and lead us to lives of unending meaning.

The three *plots*: Jesus is the true hero, and we are his story goal (his "love interest"), but he will not force us to be with him. Through repentance we can become the man or woman who learned better.

The View from the Other Side

In reducing the Scriptures to propositional statements, evangelicals have eradicated the essential conflict and resolution that lie at the heart of our story. And why have we done this? Gustaf Aulén suggests that rationalist theologians were trying to distance themselves from medieval conceptions of the devil.[17]

This is a mistake. The church would be wiser to distance itself from the actual devil than to cozy up to him by presuming he doesn't exist.

Though it may sound strange to postmodern ears, the conflict of Scripture as revealed in the gospel story is perhaps best understood not from a divine or even a human perspective, but from that of Satan. Not only does C. S. Lewis adopt this very strategy in *The Screwtape Letters*, but in *A Preface to Paradise Lost* he argues that the carnal imagination is more adapted to the nature of the villain than to that of the hero.

So what does the story of Jesus look like from the other side of the map? What is the gospel when seen from the losing side, with the chessboard turned around? Might we learn something about the mysteries of both incarnation and atonement by seeing them as Satan did, from a place of both awareness and ignorance—knowing who Jesus was but not precisely what he was up to?[18]

We can't know for sure, but the imaginative exercise is worth undertaking, with three simple disclaimers.

First, it must be stated that the church's historic anti-Semitism has no foundation or support in the gospel story. That the Jews have been targeted for hatred, exclusion, and genocide more than any other ethnic group is evidence not of their disfavor in God's eyes but of their status as God's chosen people. The target on their backs is demonic, not divine.

Second, the point of this semiotic reading of the gospel from the satanic perspective is to take in the scope of the conflict. Just as a historical fiction novel might describe the real battle of Waterloo through the eyes of a fictional character, so my retelling in the next chapter aims to use imagined details to highlight the big picture.

Third, in the account that follows I have used the second-person perspective because it's an unusual and somewhat unnerving approach, but also because I didn't want to place my readers inside Lucifer's head.

Rather, I have retold the basic arc of the life of Jesus as if we're all viewing it together as it unfolds, standing hand in hand and gazing into the darkness to ask, "Is this the man who shook the earth and made kingdoms tremble?" (Isa. 14:15–16).

12

THE GOSPEL ACCORDING TO SATAN

ACT I—Son of David

The sound of Bethlehem's bereaved women wailing in the night carried none of the usual satisfaction, none of the ironic and amusing implications of irrelevance. Their initial shrieks of rage and disbelief at the intrusion of Herod's men soon gave way to heavy-throated sobs as the merciless bloodletting of infants began, but where was *he*? That was the question. The answer, which should've been a foregone conclusion, spoiled whatever fun might have been squeezed from the moment.

Not only had the child escaped, no doubt just in the nick of time, but your reaction was prompted by panic at the realization *he* was now embodied, however small and frail, in human skin.

"Son of David" indeed! You might have known Herod's lack of subtlety would only produce the fulfillment of prophecy. *"Rachel weeping for her children and refusing to be comforted, because they are no more."*

Perhaps that couldn't be helped. But the resulting confusion among your forces was concerning. How many would need to be flogged into submission once again, making the fear of you more terrible than the fear of him—if that were possible?

Of course *he*, the Holy One, would arrive in some unexpected way, not in a palace but in a manger, stripped of even the dignity of rank. It was so like him, so pretentiously naive, so pompous in its indifference, so ugly in its false humility. He would write his own story his own way, tolerating no hero but himself, whitewashing every self-centered act as a gift of love but always taking with one hand what he had first given with the other. Wasn't life always followed by death? Hadn't he announced his own arrival as a poor child in a poor home not with messages written in the dirt but with a numberless host of enemy guardians splitting wide the night sky? And if they sang to a band of shepherds, what did that change? Were the vile flock-herders not his people, thoughtless and uneducated and easy to impress? Of course shepherds would be overawed! Would they not afterward spread the news to everyone, giving the lie to his pretense of diffidence?

Your lieutenants should've seen that this wasn't the time for a violent assault. That would come later. First he must be studied so that his weaknesses could be exposed.

What you didn't understand was what he was doing *here* and *now* in the here and now. Such an invasion—captain of the host enfolded in the flesh of an infant—was altogether too soon and too small to be believed. He must be building up to something larger and more meaningful—a coup against your own lawful rule. Something to do with the temple, his father's house, and a gathering of the "chosen people" to take back the earth for their king.

But dominion was yours. It couldn't be ripped away by force. Not by him. That sort of conquest required the cooperation of his covenant people, and Israel had long ago turned against him. They were yours now, like every other human kingdom.

So you bided your time and watched from a distance in Egypt and then in Galilee as he moved ant-like through boyhood and puberty, undistracted and unhurried, laughing and weeping and so often stopping to gaze at creation, and especially at other people, with that wordless expression you couldn't read.

He was hiding something, surely.

But could this be used? The fact he was never one of them even as a child? Or the way the people of Nazareth thought him strange and unboyish? Or that even his own brothers let you twist his compassion into scorn, so that in their imagination he wasn't the protective big brother who prayed ceaselessly for their well-being but a self-righteous tyrant who reveled in his position as "Father's favorite"?

And who better to drive that wedge inward than his mother who, knowing better, wove for him a seamless rabbinic robe but couldn't keep you from assaulting her mind with doubts about the past, the present, and the future. You made the most of the old man's words at the temple, Simeon's ringing proclamation that "a sword will pierce your own soul too," ignoring the words that preceded them, that Mary's firstborn would be—indeed, already *was*—God's "salvation."

A fool's words from the mouth of a wasted life! And who but God would ask for such sacrifice? So you knew what those words represented. You recognized their saw-toothed holiness, felt their ragged edges bite the smoke-heavy air of the temple courtyard, remembered once standing in that place of surging otherness yourself—not in the earthly copy but in the reality of the Presence, its awful inspiration.

And when he went down to the river you supposed he meant at last to launch his campaign of reclamation, that this was the beginning he had been preparing. Jesus of Nazareth, come at last to the age of a teacher, would join forces with his cousin the Baptizer and begin to retake the kingdom of Israel village by village.

Any fool might have seen it coming. But you didn't expect him to kneel in the shallow water, to subject himself to the indignity of baptism by and through a broken vessel. How could the Spirit, alighting feather-like on his shoulders, endorse this? How could the Throne speak its *pleasure*? Not merely the son of David, but "my Son, whom I love; with him I am well pleased"?

What could baptism mean to him? He'd never felt the lash of sin and separation. He'd never been rejected as a grunting, sweating, half-animal human, never suffered the awful emptiness of the outer darkness.

231

When at last you couldn't contain your rage at his presumption, you shouted into the void between worlds that this bit of theater might fool the plebes who lined the banks of the Jordan, but it did not change anything. He was no more anointed by John, no more fit for earthly kingship, than he'd been before. His baptism was a submission, not an elevation. The crown was still yours. Earth was yours. Israel was yours!

This time he heard you, as only he could, but he merely rose dripping from the stream and strode alone into the arid waste, you trailing unhurried far behind.

You would meet him in the wilderness, but on your terms, and though you understood the power at his disposal, you needed to be sure that he would not use it. Not yet. You wouldn't wrestle the whirlwind. If his sense of fair play and internal noncontradiction prevented him from responding to deception with deception, to force with force, then all was not lost. All might even be gained, or at least held indefinitely.

You trailed him until dusk, and when he stopped to rest and light a small fire, you stood in the flickering shadows so that by your presence he might find sleep impossible. Instead, he drifted off immediately.

Night turned to day and the game continued until he arrived at a stream where he built a lean-to against the sun, as if he knew what you had in mind. But he was the one limited by a human form, so you were content to wait as his spiritual filling—if indeed the ocean could be filled with water—turned to a physical emptying.

Would sonship—communion with the eternal—be enough? Even in the absence of real food, when his body began to scream its torment and turned inward to devour itself?

Forty days passed before you appeared to him there. You approached with a light step and spoke from behind him and to the left, from the position of domination. Not an accusation but a direct and sensible solution. Wasn't he human? Didn't he have needs?

"If you are the Son of God," you said, "tell these stones to become bread."

He was perched on a flat slab of rock, half in the shade of an overhanging crag, head resting on fingertips, elbows crooked against his knees, and he didn't flinch when your words cut the air. "It is written," he said, not even glancing your direction, "'Man does not live by bread alone, but on every word that comes from the mouth of God.'"

"Yes," you answered. "And is it not also written that he will command his angels concerning you? If, then, you are the Son of God, throw yourself down. Or do you not believe your own promises?"

His hair lay matted with sweat against his scalp, and his seamless robe was streaked with dust. But still he would not look at you. "It is also written: 'Do not put the Lord your God to the test.'"

You stood before him then, a few steps away, closer than you could have come in that other realm where his brilliance shone with the force of a billion suns. Then, because you knew it would get his attention, you knelt. He *would* look at you!

When he did finally look up, his eyes flashed. But those eyes were now encased in flesh, and his power lay ensconced behind the wall of his own nature.

"Earth is mine," you said. "And I can give it to you. This facade can be over. I will *give* you the children of Adam. Every nation, every tongue, every tribe. They were given to me, and I can give them to anyone I want. Why fight me over this? They aren't worth"—you gestured toward the rocks at his feet, still decidedly not bread—"*this*. All I ask is that you bow down and worship me."

For a moment he seemed to waver. Then, with surprising strength, he rose to his feet. "Enough," he said, panting with the effort. "It is written. It is *written*! 'Worship the Lord your God, and serve him only.'"

His terms, then. His claim to kingship would be based in principle rather than power.

He would abide by what was written.

And that would be his undoing.

You laughed as you flew from him deeper into the wild.

ACT II—King of the Jews

Thereafter you gave strict orders to your *shedim*, your wraiths, to announce at every confrontation his identity and therefore his claim to earthly authority: *This is the Creator, Lord of the council, the Holy One of God. Of course he demands to be obeyed!*

Your lieutenants mistook this, as you anticipated, as a strategy to challenge divine authority with divine authority. This made sense to them because it was the same case you'd been making through the ages. What you had by right from Adam was a kingly writ. But they, the lesser spirits, stupidly believed they could invoke the Name to control the One whose name it was. Their resulting humiliation was well deserved.

Meanwhile, you played the long game. If his claim to earthly dominion could be twisted so that the masses followed him for his Godness rather than his goodness, his position as ruler rather than the principles on which that authority rested, how could he claim true dominion? Wouldn't that be admitting his rule was about self-interest? Couldn't you claim that anyone who followed him because he was the Son of God, or even the son of David, was allied not with beauty, truth, and goodness, but with raw power? Hadn't all history—the tower, the flood, the plagues unleashed on Egypt—proven this point?

But he would not permit it.

From the moment he left the desert and reentered a synagogue, he refused to allow any proclamation of his true identity as Son, immediately throttling the voice of one who tried to dominate him through magic. "Everyone on the side of truth listens to me," he said once, making truth, not divinity, the central issue.

Yet his plan demanded that the earth be conquered by *Messiah* as king of Israel. And how could he be both?

It was written: Dominion came to you via Adam. Jesus would try to usurp that dominion through a covenant based on faith. That is, an individual's rejection of the natural earthly order for a higher state of dominion. Humans could appeal to the higher laws of the divine council.

But they were all lawbreakers. Which meant they were trapped between the two states, and nothing would change that until your own dominion could be stripped away. Every person acquiesced at some point. All sinned. All submitted themselves to your rule. Even Israel had turned away. Which made his incarnation puzzling.

Why journey to the region of the Gerasenes to confront Legion, a captain of no small ability? Shouldn't the Christ's jurisdiction have ended when he stepped from the boat? Yet the force of his deliverance slaughtered a herd of pigs!

It wasn't until he went to Tyre to exorcise an independent from the daughter of a gentile woman that you understood he was re-creating, reliving, the Scriptures. Your personal duel with him in the wilderness had mirrored the exile from Egypt. His sermon on the mountainside proclaimed himself a new and improved Moses. And this Canaanite woman matched and perfected the moment Elijah came to Zarephath asking for bread.

The message this sent grew clearer. Not content to reform his chosen people, he was reaching into the nations where long ago he had given the now-freed watchers territorial authority. He was picking a fight. Provoking you. *Come and get me!*

He would build his church, and the gates of hell would not prevail against it. Jesus of Nazareth planned to drive you out just as he drove out the Amorites through his namesake, Joshua. He was building to a physical conquest.

Your lieutenants wanted to kill him immediately, but you prevented them. Jesus of Nazareth was the tree of life. Death wouldn't stop him unless the whole tree could be uprooted and cast out. Before Jesus could be killed, he had to be anointed as king and then rejected by his people. If you could do that, you would remove the Holy One's foothold on earth permanently.

Meanwhile you watched as he invited women and lepers into his closest circle. You listened as he issued absurd demands regarding lust and anger and even harsher demands about loving one's neighbor. When he multiplied food, you multiplied the expectations of the crowds. When he healed their bodies, you scarred their minds. When he drove out your wraiths, you found them new hosts in more strategic locations.

Did he know you had someone on the inside, a man among his closest disciples? Did he understand there wasn't a single disciple you couldn't turn when the time came? And with only the slightest bit of pressure—a mocking laugh, the ridicule of a maiden, the coin of a Pharisee?

Even after the whole of Judea seemed to know his name, he had nothing to show for it besides the calluses on his feet and the scorn of his elders. And if all the pressure you brought to bear through the circumstances of his itinerant teaching and healing didn't pierce his armor, well, you hadn't really expected it to. You knew him from of old. The point of stirring up petty betrayals and backstabbing gossip was never to break him. It was to hurt him. A splinter under the nail could be more satisfying than an open wound. This was your power, the power of attrition. You had no foothold in the Christ, but he had no foothold in the world. After three years of grasping at the wind his hands were still empty.

Even so, how confident his words were! And how often he spoke in riddles, darting his taunts in four directions at once: to the crowds, to the scribes, to the disciples, and last of all to you. The curious masses, who so often delighted in his parables, gleaned nothing that might have freed them from you. But they did delight when his stories robbed the scribes and Pharisees of their dignity!

You took advantage of this, elevating him in the minds of both groups—in reality a delightful demotion—to the status of an entertainer, conjurer, political zealot, rabble-rouser, or conquering general.

When he told a story about two men, one wealthy and the other a poor beggar named Lazarus, you made the story an affront to the dignity of the teachers of the law, pointing out that they had worked hard for their money and positions. With the underclasses you exaggerated the importance of money as a sign of vice and encouraged their resentment. Poverty *itself* was a moral good; there was no need to share the little one had with someone who had less.

When he spoke of a man who sowed good seed in his field only to discover that an enemy had sowed weeds overnight, you enticed both the crowd and the self-righteous elites to see *themselves* as the sowers of good seed. In this way they missed the point entirely, blinding themselves to your presence as the sower of weeds and placing themselves in the forbidden seat of judgment. Some of them walked away even more self-righteous than before, as if the story only affirmed the wickedness of their least favorite neighbors.

At times the twisting of his words was made all too easy by his own exacting perfection. A less scrupulous but more canny orator might have chosen as their hero a common laborer or middle-class Jew rather than a Samaritan. But Jesus of Nazareth set up as the standard of right behavior a hated enemy and made the villains of his tale a priest and a Levite. It was child's play to suggest that he had crossed a moral line and set himself up as an agent of foreign gods or a political ally of Israel's enemies. Was he suggesting that even a Samaritan, even a *Roman*, might find favor with the God of Israel? Worse, did he mean that everyone owed a debt of covenantal hesed—of lovingkindness—to every person they encountered? Outrageous!

How ironic that his parable of the sower so clearly delineated what was happening, yet still they missed it—thanks to you! Your "birds" were ever ready to snatch from the mind any seed that might sprout into an awareness of moral degeneracy or spiritual doom. Even the more difficult targets eventually yielded to the pressures of work or family rejection or sexual frustration. If not, there was always the oh-so-satisfying pressure of pleasure, of twisting a good out of context and out of bounds until it became a destructive force.

But you understood the implications of that parable. And you knew that he understood your understanding.

Perhaps that was why his stories became more barbed, more layered in their capacity to strike not just at the hearts of the common and the elevated but at you.

There were times when the force of his pronouncements made your scales ripple in agitation. He spoke as if he knew not just what you were thinking but what you were *incapable* of thinking. And this was maddening.

If "it is written" were to be fair, then it must be comprehensive. It must include everything. What then had you missed?

"The kingdom of heaven is like treasure hidden in a field," he said once. "When a man found it, he hid it again, and then in his joy went away and sold all he had and bought that field." You knew who the man was. You recognized the field as the whole earth under your dominion. But what had he hidden? And what right did he have to be joyful? He was not winning. And he had turned down your offer to sell it back to him. How then would he make such a purchase if not through the blood of his followers, the nation of Israel marching again to war under Yeshua, but this Yeshua unhindered by a tainted bloodline and the internal chaos of your influence?

You saw it most clearly when he stood in the courtyard of the temple, wreathed in a band of sunlight swirling with dust, his presence so filling the place that the people inside were drawn to gather around him. *God was a landowner who had planted a vineyard and rented it to some farmers*, he said.

The elders were there, of course, but they didn't understand that he was looking at you when he said, "Last of all, he sent his son to them. 'They will respect my son,' he said. But when the tenants saw the son, they said to each other, 'This is the heir. Come, let's kill him and take his inheritance.' So they took him and threw him out of the vineyard and killed him. Therefore, when the owner of the vineyard comes, what will he do to those tenants?"

The idiot priests, who didn't understand the story at first, responded with the obvious: "He will bring those wretches to a wretched end."

But he was still looking at you, and in the silence that followed, as the elites recognized their own damnation, you understood your victory. If you killed him, he would simply return in power to forcibly remove your claim on earth's kingdoms.

This was the first truly shocking thing you heard him say. For where then would his precious holiness be? If he couldn't persuade humanity to follow him because of his so-called goodness, would he really just tip over the board and storm away?

Still, you didn't quite believe it until, leaving the temple and the city, he said to his disciples, "If the owner of the house had known at what time of night the thief was coming, he would have kept watch and would not have let his house be broken into."

You were the owner of that house! And now he planned to come as a thief in the night, supported by enforcers from the Throne, to rob you of a dominion you had no reason to surrender.

At last he'd admitted that his justice was merely another word for power. At last he'd revealed his weakness and hypocrisy. The random misery of life, the cruelty of existence in a plane of cosmic indifference, had finally worn down even the Holy One.

Soon, the chief priests must be persuaded to reject their king. Then and only then—but also *immediately* then—he must be executed under the law. Everything must be legal. Was it not written? Was it not all recorded in advance? Was that not the law?

Once, you tried to make him king by force, by way of a crowd worked to a frenzy by your agents. But he knew what you were planning and removed himself before the plot could gain traction.

Very well. You were patient. And when you began to sense the nearness of the moment in the swelling crowds of people who gathered at Jerusalem for Passover, you handled the matter personally. You knew the Scriptures and you knew what to look for. If you couldn't make him king, then you would seize the moment he chose for himself. You would recognize what even his disciples might miss. Just as everything else in his life had been upside down—born in a manger, apprenticed to a carpenter, baptized by a madman—so too his anointing as king would also be inverted.

And indeed he *had* to be anointed, for was it not written? He must ride into Jerusalem on the back of a donkey, but riding wasn't enough. He must ride in as a king certified by the Throne. It wasn't sufficient to be *announced* as king, for hadn't even one of David's sons been proclaimed and yet deposed? No, Jesus of Nazareth would have to be anointed as king before he could declare himself.

The moment came in Bethany, in the house of Simon the leper, as Jesus reclined with his disciples and with Lazarus, the one he'd raised from the dead. All the elements were present, both for the precedent stories of King Saul, King David, King Solomon, and King Jehu, as well as for their messianic inversions.

When the woman, Mary, the sister of Lazarus, entered the guest room with her jar of rare spikenard and broke it open to lavish it on his feet, you hesitated. Everything about the moment screamed divinity, humility, and *kairos*. But it wasn't until she moved the jar from his feet to his head, tipping out the fragrant sticky oil so that it streamed down his hair and face, that you knew.

The Ancient of Days had anointed Jesus of Nazareth as king of Israel. At the hand of a woman. In the house of a leper.

The Throne had endorsed him at last. Which meant that everything was now legal.

It was written!

The woman thought she was preparing him for burial, because of course she believed him when he said he would be raised to life. But only you caught the double meaning in his response, his affirmation of the beauty of her faith and the fate her obedience to the Spirit would bring upon him: she *was* preparing his body for burial. To a real king, death and kingship were synonymous.

The woman didn't understand this, nor could the disciples. Perhaps Lazarus, having tasted death, might have understood, but at the moment he was thinking only of his astonishment at sitting alive in the Presence.

The moment was lost to all of them, highlighting the Messiah's loneliness. His resurrection would be meaningless without the chosen people. And he would not have them, because you would not *let* him have them. A king without a kingdom? A kingdom without a king?

Only he, the Christ, the anointed one, understood this, and the pain of betrayal that lined his face was, in that moment, sublime. He saw you whisper your offense in Judas's ear: *Should not this perfume have been sold and the money given to the poor?*

ACT III—Thief

You were ready for the moment. Everything had been arranged beforehand, so it wasn't difficult to set the cart rolling downhill. Pontius Pilate had long ago surrendered so much of his humanity to your control that he was now little more than a puppet dancing on your strings. Caiaphas was a more interesting subject and would need a lighter touch, but you knew you could count on his influence to sway the elders who might vacillate on matters of law.

The people of Israel were another matter. Not because they were any different from Adam's other descendants—that sea of sweating hobgoblins—but because they'd been chosen by him. Any crowd, given the right provocation, could be transformed into a soulless mob. But what if you weren't the only one manipulating them? Might the Throne claim its own covenant rights and indulge in a manipulation you couldn't match—just as he'd done with Moses back in Egypt? What if his staff once again swallowed those of your puppet rulers?

It was Passover, after all, and surely that fact was significant to him. If only you knew why!

But you didn't know, so you waited until the story was told again during the Passover Seder, Jesus recalling each event with characteristic insight and wit—as if he had lived the story himself. When he came to the part where the court magicians flung down their staves, you entered Judas, transforming him from something like polished deadwood to a living serpent. What would the Christ do now? Would he swallow up his own disciple?

Instead he gave a short, ambiguous command: "What you are about to do, do quickly."

You of course complied, for things must happen quickly at this point.

First the arrangements for his betrayal, the silver paid out, the soldiers and officials sent from the chief priests and Pharisees, Jesus already in torment in the garden. Clearly he knew he had already lost and was making arrangements with the Throne to burn up the law and attack the earth in force. Not another flood, unless he meant to go back on

241

that promise too, but perhaps a sea of fire consuming the brokenness of his creation. Another admission of failure.

Then a show trial conducted by Annas and the chief priests under the cover of darkness in the early hours of the morning. Only those elites fully under the control of your wraiths were summoned. Meanwhile, a small beating coupled with baseless accusations would create anxiety and send the message that more, so much more, would have to be endured. You wouldn't make this easy. He had invaded your world, after all. This was his idea.

Another trial, this time before Caiaphas, and the caginess of the high priest's insight convinced those elders who were still reluctant that Jesus of Nazareth was just one man, after all, and wasn't it better for one man to die than for the Romans to burn down their nation?

Then at last, as the sun began to rise, the soldiers stood him before Pilate. You were quick to point out the strong odor trailing after him, the smell of spikenard, the aroma of royalty. And if he didn't *look* like a king, was that not so much more an offense to the mind, if not to Rome?

"Are you the king of the Jews?" Pilate asked.

"Is that your own idea," Jesus asked, "or did others talk to you about me?"

"Am I a Jew?" Pilate replied, because of course it was you who had been talking to him all along and Jesus knew this. But you needed to press the point, to make it extremely and undeniably clear *why* he was being killed. When he claimed that his kingdom was that of another world, you made Pilate put the question bluntly: "You are a king, then!"

Jesus of Nazareth wouldn't lie to save himself. "You are right in saying I am a king."

From this point forward it was crucial that everything be executed with crystalline clarity. You ushered Pilate out in front of the chosen people, who had already been stirred up by your skilled agents, and put the very words into his mouth: "I find no basis for a charge against him. But it is your custom for me to release to you one prisoner at the time of the Passover. Do you want me to release 'the king of the Jews'?"

Two prisoners—Jesus, Son of the Father and anointed king, and the robber, Barabbas—were presented to the crowd. When they demanded that you release Barabbas, you delayed, ordering instead that Jesus be flogged. This after all would be your first, and likely your only, opportunity to do to him what you had so often desired. More importantly, the point must be driven home again and again, not for the sake of the people but for the sake of the divine council. If his people rejected him as king, what foothold could he claim on earth? What right did he have to rule? Earth did not *want* him!

He returned staggering, his back flayed open, the wounds seeping in streaks into the purple robe you'd prepared in anticipation of this moment. Your soldiers had pressed a crown of thorns into his scalp and the blood streamed around his swollen face.

"I find no basis for a charge against him," Pilate said.

Humans were so predictable. Your denial only sent them into a frothing rage. Now they demanded crucifixion. But Pilate, as instructed, refused. Again they demanded crucifixion, this time appealing to their own law and the fact that Jesus had claimed to be the Son of God.

The beauty of all this was that the trial wasn't just a mockery, it was an honest mockery. Nothing aroused your pride more than your ability to deceive with facts, to tell just enough of the truth that whatever remained hidden didn't seem to matter. So when Pilate again and again tried to set Jesus free, the people only grew more insistent. And your case against the Throne was made.

Sitting down, Pilate reiterated the plain facts of the case, the dilemma of dominion, one last time: "Here is your king."

"We have no king but Caesar," the chief priests answered.

And that was all you needed. Pilate handed him over to be crucified so that he would be not only rejected but cursed, and over his head you ordered that a sign be fastened to remind the Throne that all humanity—even his own people—had rejected him: "Jesus of Nazareth, the king of the Jews."

On Golgotha they crucified him between two thieves, which was fitting since he had come as a thief and taken the place of a thief and even planned to return as a thief.

You stood by and watched as the hours ticked away and the men on the crosses groaned. When Jesus recited the "My God, my God" psalm, you started to worry, for it hadn't occurred to you that this obscure reflection on David's life might have resonance here. But when six hours later he cried out, "It is finished," you breathed a sigh of relief.

He was dead, and even the rocks cried out in protest and the temple veil split and the sun went dark. But you reveled in the darkness.

He was dead! The Holy One of Israel had surrendered himself to you and lost earth forever!

He was dead he was dead he was dead!

Victory secured, you soared above the city and perched on the roof of the temple to ponder what might happen next. Would the sky roll back to reveal a vanguard of archangels? Would your own forces, with nowhere left to hide, slowly be destroyed?

Or might even the archangels hesitate? How loyal would Michael and the hosts of heaven be, seeing the true nature of the Holy One who was no longer holy? Would Gabriel continue to serve the God who had at last declared himself to be not the origin of deep mysteries but the strong arm of entitlement?

As you gazed out across the city, you recalled your confrontation in the wilderness. He should have accepted your offer. You would have given him all this, all the kingdoms of the earth, to see him bow down and worship you. And now what did he have?

All the kingdoms of the world were yours. You had dominion over *all* of it. You could do with it as you pleased, unless and until he pried it from your hands by force, and contrary to the nature of the law.

The earthquake had shattered walls and collapsed roofs. Beneath you, the sound of weeping began to rise from the rubble. Torchlight flickered to life down in the streets, and you sensed the indignity and horror of the Levites inside the temple under your feet.

Recognition began its slow boil in your chest as you saw that earth had, for the moment, become your domain metaphorically as well as literally. You had long been satisfied with the absence of light. Deep darkness, the unpredictability and unknowability of chaos, where nothing was known or could be known except the self, had followed in your wake ever since you fled the Presence. Hell was home to you, and home was hell. You were remaking earth in your image.

This was your world, not his. He had no place in it. The fool!

But then, if he had no place in it, why had he allowed himself to be taken so easily? Why had he given up his life as if it were nothing?

You could see him still hanging there on the cross, on the place of the skull beyond the city walls. It was not his world. Why had he come for it?

Slowly the horror of realization took you as you began at last to see the consequences of your own logic. Your gloating turned to panic and then to blinding rage.

You had said that this was your world, not his. *He had no place in it.* But if he had no place in it, what right did you have to kill him?

Then, as you stared out across the darkness of the city, thrones were set in place and the Ancient of Days took his seat. A river of fire was flowing, coming out from before him. The courts were seated and the books were opened. You could see it happening in your mind's eye as clearly as if you were there, standing before the council.

The voice that spoke into your darkness was like a thousand voices united in one, like the roar of water tumbling down a mountainside: "Now the prince of this world will be driven out."

You were still crouching on the roof of the temple, but a weight had descended on your shoulders, the weight of the world, and before you could respond, the weight pressed you flat against the surface to gaze into the black courtyard below. You opened your mouth to speak but the crushing heaviness stole the breath from your lungs. Instead, you flung accusations from your mind like flaming sulfur: *You deceived me! How can you, the Holy One, deceive?*

Power like a billion butterflies swarmed around you. Something like a garment was stripped from you, and when it fluttered free you saw that it looked like a scroll with writing on both sides, sealed with the witness of the eternal Spirit.

"You have deceived yourself."

You snarled, the only resistance left to you. *Earth is mine! The kingdoms are mine! Dominion is mine!*

A second voice, this one like the passing of a distant breeze, said, "The other beasts have been stripped of their authority, but they will be allowed to live for a period of time."

The weight lifted slowly, almost reluctantly, and for just a moment you seemed to be staring into the brilliance of the Throne. But it was just the sun emerging from its long eclipse.

"Is it not written," a third voice asked, "'only spare his life'?"

"And is it not written," added the second, "'In that day, the LORD will punish with his sword—his fierce, great and powerful sword—'"

But you knew what was coming before you heard it.

You knew because you knew that sword, the sword of his word.

It is written!

"Leviathan the gliding serpent, Leviathan the coiling serpent; he will slay the monster of the sea."

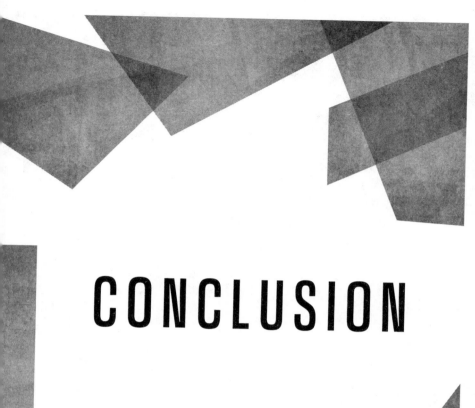

CONCLUSION

13

ONE TRUE STORY

We are image bearers. Like it or not, *intend* it or not, you and I and every other human who ever lived has reflected, directly and indirectly, the divine image in which we were made. One need not be religious to fulfill this purpose for life. The man who rescues a drowning cat from a flooded river has acted out the image of the Creator who loves and serves creation. The agnostic nurse who administers CPR to someone suffering a heart attack shines forth the nature of the "God of the living." The old man who tells stories to his delighted grandchildren images something both human and divine, something eternal.

Stories also bear the human and the divine images, even when they aren't trying to—even when they're broken or poorly conceived or thematically hostile to God. A story that works as a story reflects, at its most basic level, the meaning of existence.

The Bible is the clearest example of this principle, though like humans it often buries its more difficult revelations so deep that only those who sit at the feet of Jesus will ever find them. Perhaps that's why so many have forgotten that the center of our faith isn't a set of doctrines or propositional truths but a story—the story of Jesus.

In their book *The Drama of Scripture*, authors Craig Bartholomew and Michael Goheen note the depth of our disconnection from our faith's central story:

> Australian sociologist John Carroll, who does not profess to be a Christian, believes that the reason that the church in the West is in trouble is because it has forgotten its story. In his view the "waning of Christianity as practiced in the West is easy to explain. The Christian churches have comprehensively failed in their one central task—to retell their foundation story in a way that might speak to the times."[1]

Recapturing a deeper understanding of that story will take time and effort and the humility to admit that we have much to learn. Still, we have the covenantal promise of God's help as we seek to learn from him. He wants to teach us, to respond to our cries for deeper understanding.

I'm often asked how a nonacademic might begin a deeper study of Scripture when so much seems confusing or fit primarily for scholars and historians. My response is twofold.

First, remember that the stories of the Bible were designed to be listened to. There is nothing wrong with reading them silently to oneself, but regularly listening to an audiobook version can be startlingly revelatory. Things you miss when scanning the text visually—connections between semiotic signposts—may jump out at you with unexpected clarity.

Second, try to consume larger sections than you're used to reading, avoiding the traditional chapter breaks and instead paying attention to the places where a narrative arc seems to come to a natural resolution. The goal is to defamiliarize the text and read/hear it as if for the first time. In short, read for the story rather than for any propositions or doctrines you've been taught to filter Scripture through. Stories, after all, reveal both the nature of human existence and the nature of the personal/relational God of Scripture.

The vault at the center of the Bible is Jesus—Jesus the fulfillment of the story of Israel. Jesus the salvation of humanity, who by his blood purchased people for God. Jesus the ruler who robbed Satan of his corrupt authority and reigns forevermore. Jesus the "true human" who shows us what we are called to in the final restoration of all things when heaven and earth will again be united.

The vault at the center of the human soul is the inner holy place where God desires to take up residence as our treasure in these "jars of clay" (2 Cor. 4:7). Christ is the answer to the despair of Solomon that the meaning of life cannot be known from the material universe. Christ is the answer to the despair of every human heart that longs for reality to make sense, for life with all its tragic surprises and shattered expectations to mean something bigger and more important than just eating and drinking and making merry, for tomorrow we die.

Story Ending

During my doctoral studies, my eighty-four-year-old mother fell in her apartment and had to be taken to the hospital. The circumstances of that fall were a little weird, for she didn't seem hurt by it. But my brother, calling her via a video phone, saw her lying on the tiled floor.

"What are you doing, Mom?"

"Oh, just lying here."

"Are you okay?"

"Yes."

At this point he was already calling for an ambulance because she seemed "spacey," and he feared she'd hit her head on the tiles. The paramedics found her still lying there, the walker upright at her feet. She had no visible marks on her head or back, but it appeared she'd tipped backward and slammed into the floor without attempting to brace herself. They asked for, and received, permission to take her to the hospital to check for internal injury.

I heard the story when her bloodwork came back indicating she had a very aggressive form of leukemia that would likely take her life in a matter of weeks. I immediately headed for the hospital, a thirty-minute drive, and by the time I got there she'd already agreed to start treatment.

Because this happened while COVID protocols were in place, we were only allowed in her room one at a time. I entered just as the doctor was explaining that they'd ordered an ambulance to take her to a different location, a research hospital, to begin the chemo.

"Mom," I said, "I'm with you, and I know Barbara and Barney and Dave are with you too if you choose to fight for your life. I don't blame you. But has the doctor explained what will happen if you agree to this? Has she explained the likely outcome of the treatment?"

"No," she said. "They just said there's only one way to beat it."

My mom was an educated person, a nurse with two degrees and a lifetime of experience in the medical industry. That she hadn't gotten the whole picture alarmed me.

"This treatment requires isolation. It kills more than half of the people who receive it and has never saved the life of anyone over sixty. Mom, it has a *zero percent chance* of saving your life, and if you sign the papers, you will be whisked away to another hospital where you won't be able to see anyone—your kids, your grandkids, your friends, your pastor. Statistically, it's a death sentence, and in a place where you won't have anyone you know to be with you. Is this really what you want?"

This was difficult news to deliver. I watched her expression turn to sheer terror as she realized there was no good option. While she'd believed there was a chance to live, she'd held on to that hope as to a lifeline. But I'd stripped that away.

I sat next to her. For a long time we listened to the clicking and beeping of machines that measured the various malfunctions of her dying body.

"God caught me when I fell," she said at last.

Thinking I'd misunderstood her, I said, "What?"

My mother and I had a long history of disagreement over the nature of reality, particularly regarding God's place in the universe. She, the daughter of a Lutheran minister, had always seemed to believe that God wasn't just predictably distant but decidedly Lutheran. When in college I'd described my encounter with Christ and spiritual rebirth, she hadn't seemed to take it seriously. I was in a phase. I would grow out of it. I would come to my senses. If I wanted to serve God, I would do it the right way and enter Lutheran seminary. Though these opinions softened over the years, she never really seemed to accept my conviction that God still moves in the lives of his people, that he isn't out there a million miles away but right here beside us and in us and intimately involved in the daily affairs of our lives, however broken they may seem. To my mother, "God with us" really meant something like "God is *for* us, generally speaking."

Thus my surprise when she said a second time, and even more emphatically, "God! *Caught* me! When I *fell*!"

Still perplexed (and whose turn was it to be the doubting one now?), I said, "You mean, like, an angel or something? There was someone behind you?"

"I was walking into the bathroom and I felt myself falling backward," she said. "Straight back. And when I was halfway

253

down, hands caught me in midair and lowered me gently to the floor."

"But you didn't see anyone?"

This time she wagged an arthritic finger at me. "God caught me."

"I believe you," I said. "It's just a weird story. But yeah. I believe you."

"I knew you would. That's why I told you."

Then, as I watched, the fear returned and I saw that she was still dealing with the recognition there was no way out for her. I had seen my mother cry many times, but I had never seen her terrified.

"What's going to happen to me?" she whispered.

"Mom," I said, not knowing what to say but feeling the need to open my mouth, even if I had no wise or comforting words. She needed me to say something, to remind her she wasn't alone. "I don't know how much longer you have. It doesn't seem like you have much time left. But I can tell you this: when the end comes, the same God who caught you in the bathroom will catch you again in every way that matters."

She passed away two and a half weeks later in her own apartment, surrounded by family. I can't say that her death was pain-free. But I never again saw that expression of terror. And looking back, it has often struck me that God is a marvelous storyteller. He knows how to end a story. He even knows how to turn an ending into a beginning.

No matter how broken or misaligned the puzzle of your life, Jesus can fit it seamlessly into the flow of his. No life is truly small. No story is insignificant. No one who comes to him in humility will ever be turned away.

The story of Jesus is the one true story that gives meaning to all the others. Which is why the language of that story is not just the language of humanity; it is the language of life.

The Spirit and the bride say, "Come!" And let the one who hears say, "Come!" Let the one who is thirsty come; and let the one who wishes take the free gift of the water of life.

Revelation 22:17

ACKNOWLEDGMENTS

Shortly before he died, Thomas Aquinas reportedly called all that he'd written a heap of straw. That "heap" was at least written by Thomas Aquinas. If *my* heap can be recommended, it's only thanks to the hard work of many other people who helped shape it.

I am indebted to Brian Vos, Amy Nemecek, and everyone at Baker Books who believed in and contributed to this project.

Special thanks is owed to my agent, Steve Laube, for more than just the advice and encouragement you've provided on this and my other projects. I am amazed at how supportive you are of the oddball writers who throw manuscripts your way. Thank you for believing in the wild and wonderful beauty of an untamed Creator.

I'm also deeply grateful to my doctoral committee: Dr. Tony Blair, Tineke Hegeman Bryson, and Dr. Timothy R. Valentino. Thank you for your insight into making *The God of Story* better, for pushing me to rethink and revise and reimagine, and for reminding me that "even the DMins believe, and they tremble."

Dr. Leonard Sweet gave me invaluable feedback and encouragement on many of these chapters, which were in some cases submitted as papers for the semiotics track at Kairos University. For two years you told me frankly what did and didn't work, and I'm certain I would not have embraced the ubuntu of God without your influence. For that and for many other things, thank you!

My fellow griffins, Jim Allen and Justin Scoggins, provided comic relief as well as excellent pushback on some of my zanier ideas. I'm amazed and delighted that our miscreant friendship has continued after seminary.

Thanks to Rachel Garner, Jared Schmitz, and Rosey Mucklestone, beta readers who provided helpful feedback and encouragement. You are a refreshing reminder that theology is not an exclusive hobby but the domain of real people who walk with God in often uncelebrated ways.

Mike and Pam Jensen and everyone at the house church where I worship were routinely supportive. Thank you for praying for this project and tolerating my numerous rants about obscure theological discussions.

And finally, to my wife, Carrol, for putting up with my recurring bouts of self-doubt and for deepening many of my "What if?" propositions with profound insights of your own. Thank you for sharing the journey of life with me. I could ask for no better companion.

NOTES

Foreword

1. John F. Kennedy, "Address at American University, June 10, 1963," in vol. 3 of *Public Papers of the Presidents of the United States: John F. Kennedy* (Washington, DC: US Government Printing Office, 1964), 502–6.

2. Frederick Buechner, *The Remarkable Ordinary: How to Stop, Look, and Listen to Life* (Grand Rapids: Zondervan, 2017), 47.

3. Buechner, *The Remarkable Ordinary*, 53.

Chapter 1 The Great Pyramid

1. Melanie C. Green and Timothy C. Brock, "The Role of Transportation in the Persuasiveness of Public Narratives," *Journal of Personality and Social Psychology* 79, no. 5 (2000): 701.

2. Leonard Sweet, *The Bad Habits of Jesus: Showing Us the Way to Live Right in a World Gone Wrong* (Carol Stream, IL: Tyndale, 2016), 77.

3. Jonathan Gottschall, *The Storytelling Animal: How Stories Make Us Human* (New York: Mariner Books, 2013), 55.

4. Mark Lehner and Zahi Hawass, *Giza and the Pyramids: The Definitive History* (Chicago: University of Chicago Press, 2017), 91.

5. Gottschall, *The Storytelling Animal*, 58.

6. Gottschall, *The Storytelling Animal*, 52.

7. C. S. Lewis, *Of Other Worlds* (New York: HarperOne, 2017), 60.

8. Diana Wynne Jones, *Reflections: On the Magic of Writing* (New York: Greenwillow Books, 2012), 78.

9. Maria Tatar, *The Annotated Classic Fairy Tales* (New York: W. W. Norton & Company, 2002), 56.

10. Leonard Sweet and Michael Adam Beck, *Contextual Intelligence: Unlocking the Ancient Secret to Mission on the Front Lines* (Oviedo, FL: HigherLife Development Services, Inc., 2020), 47–48.

11. Eugene Peterson, *Leap Over a Wall: Earthy Spirituality for Everyday Christians* (New York: HarperOne, 1998), 4.

12. James Bryan Smith, *The Magnificent Story: Uncovering a Gospel of Beauty, Goodness, and Truth* (Downers Grove, IL: InterVarsity, 2017), 4.

13. Sweet, *Bad Habits of Jesus*, 77.

Chapter 2 The Storyteller's Parable

1. Leonard Sweet, *Giving Blood: A Fresh Paradigm for Preaching* (Grand Rapids: Zondervan, 2014), 25.

2. Sweet, *Bad Habits of Jesus*, 77.

3. Sweet and Beck, *Contextual Intelligence*, 121.

4. "Elon Musk: Neuralink, AI, Autopilot, and the Pale Blue Dot," *Lex Fridman Podcast*, episode 49, November 12, 2019, https://www.youtube.com/watch?v=smK9dgdTl40&t=1088s.

5. Leonard Sweet, *The Gospel According to Starbucks: Living with a Grande Passion* (Colorado Springs: WaterBrook, 2008), 112.

6. Brian Anse Patrick, *The Ten Commandments of Propaganda* (London: Arktos, 2013), 44.

7. Sweet, *Giving Blood*, 82.

8. Michael Polanyi, *Personal Knowledge: Towards a Post-Critical Philosophy* (Chicago: University of Chicago Press, 2015), 281.

Chapter 3 The Best Theme Park Ever

1. Leland Ryken, *How Bible Stories Work: A Guided Study of Biblical Narrative* (Bellingham, WA: Lexham Press, 2015), 14.

2. Ryken, *How Bible Stories Work*, 26.

3. Karen Swallow Prior, *On Reading Well: Finding the Good Life through Great Books* (Grand Rapids: Brazos, 2018), 29.

4. William Shakespeare, *As You Like It*, act 2, scene 7.

5. Crystal L. Downing, *Changing Signs of Truth: A Christian Introduction to the Semiotics of Communication* (Downers Grove, IL: InterVarsity, 2012), 240.

6. C. S. Lewis, *The Screwtape Letters* (New York: HarperCollins, 1996), 161.

7. Jean Leclercq, *The Love of Learning and the Desire for God: A Study of Monastic Culture* (New York: Fordham University Press, 1961), 76.

Chapter 4 An Ideal World

1. Robert Alter, *Genesis: Translation and Commentary* (New York: W. W. Norton, 1996), 11–12.

2. For a deep explanation of the divine council, see Michael S. Heiser, *The Unseen Realm: Recovering the Supernatural Worldview of the Bible* (Bellingham, WA: Lexham Press, 2015). Heiser writes, "God has an unseen family—in fact, it's his original family" (25).

3. Stephen J. Vicchio explains: "The Hebrew expression *bene ha Elohim* literally means 'the sons of God.' The word *ben* is used in the Hebrew Bible not only to describe the family of a person, but also his intimate relations. Various nicknames use the word *ben*, like 'son of strength,' 'son of wickedness.' In another context, all human beings are sons of God, or children of God, as Deut 14:50 and Exod 4:22 imply." Stephen J. Vicchio, *The Book of Job: A History of Interpretation and a Commentary* (Eugene, OR: Wipf & Stock, 2020), 50.

4. Madeleine L'Engle, *Walking on Water: Reflections on Faith & Art* (New York: Convergent Books, 1980), 72.

5. See, for instance, Todd W. Hall, *Relational Spirituality: A Psychological-Theological Paradigm for Transformation* (Downers Grove, IL: InterVarsity, 2021), 104.

6. C. S. Lewis, *The Lion, the Witch and the Wardrobe* (London: Harper-Collins Children's Books, 2010), 165.

Chapter 5 The Road to Relevance

1. William Shakespeare, *Macbeth*, act 5, scene 5, lines 22–31.

2. Shakespeare, *Macbeth*, act 1, scene 3, lines 135–38.

3. Ilia Gurliand, "Reminiscences of A.P. Chekhov," *Teatr i Iskusstvo*, July 11, 1904, 521.

4. Owen Barfield, *Saving the Appearances: A Study in Idolatry*, 2nd ed. (Middletown, CT: Wesleyan University Press, 1988), 94–95.

5. Jeremy Adams, *Hollowed Out: A Warning about America's Next Generation* (Washington, DC: Regnery Publishing, 2021), 4.

6. Samuel Taylor Coleridge, "The Rime of the Ancient Mariner (text of 1834)," https://www.poetryfoundation.org/poems/43997/the-rime-of-the-ancient-mariner-text-of-1834.

7. L'Engle, *Walking on Water*, 95.

8. Iain McGilchrist, *The Master and His Emissary: The Divided Brain and the Making of the Western World* (New Haven: Yale University Press, 2019), 128.

9. *The Journals and Papers of Gerard Manley Hopkins*, ed. Humphrey House and Graham Storey (London: Oxford University Press, 1959), 84.

10. Carl Ellis and Karen Ellis, "Foreword," in William Edgar, *A Supreme Love: The Music of Jazz and the Hope of the Gospel* (Downers Grove, IL: InterVarsity, 2022), ix.

11. Dorothy L. Sayers, *The Mind of the Maker: The Expression of Faith through Creativity and Art* (New York: Open Road Media, 2015), 37.

12. I refer here to Heraclitus's conception of the *logos* as that which brings two opposites together, as a string unites the ends of a stick to make a bow.

13. Vern S. Poythress coined the term "symphonic theology" to describe the presence of parallel meanings in Scripture.

Chapter 6 Behold a Wonderful Hippo!

1. Robert Alter, *The Wisdom Books: Job, Proverbs, and Ecclesiastes* (New York: W. W. Norton, 2010), xv.

2. Consider Matthew 16:19 as rendered in Young's Literal Translation: "Whatever thou mayest bind upon earth shall be having been bound in the heavens, and whatever thou mayest loose upon the earth shall be having been loosed in the heavens."

3. David A. Dorsey, *The Literary Structure of the Old Testament: A Commentary on Genesis–Malachi* (Grand Rapids: Baker Academic, 1999), 19.

4. Dorsey, *Literary Structure*, 31.

5. Dorsey, *Literary Structure*, 170.

6. Dorsey, *Literary Structure*, 16.

7. Dorsey, *Literary Structure*, 16.

8. Sweet, *Giving Blood*, 28.

9. Stephen J. Vicchio tells us, "Gregory the Great and Thomas Aquinas both continued the Christian view that Satan and the devil were one and the same figures. . . . Henry Cowles, in his 1877 commentary, tells us: 'The Satan's character and work as put here are in full accord with the numerous allusions made to him throughout Scripture. He is the same old serpent, the Devil.'" Vicchio, *Book of Job*, 52.

10. See Deuteronomy 32:8.

11. See Luke 4:5–6.

12. Some assume God granted permission for Satan to kill Job's children, but the story doesn't suggest this. We're told Job is worried about the spiritual condition of his children, who are adults living outside his household. It's more likely we're meant to dread what's coming—that Satan has waited for an opportune time to deliver the really crushing blow of death to Job's children. Such a reading makes sense of the opening prologue and Job's reaction to the horrifying news: what he dreaded most was not the loss of his riches but the loss of his children while they were partying.

13. It would be a mistake to dismiss the narrative as anti-feminist because the words of Job's wife are intended to be seen as another twisting of the knife. Job's wife isn't the devil. It's possible she senses that the only thing keeping Job alive is his loyalty to God, and her words to him in verse 9, "Are you still holding on to your integrity? Curse God and die!" are spoken through tears of misguided but very human compassion. The Hebrew translated as "curse God" can also be translated as "bless God."

14. Malcolm Muggeridge, *The End of Christendom* (Grand Rapids: Eerdmans, 1980), 39.

15. Muggeridge, *The End of Christendom*, 40.
16. See, for instance, Job 4:8–9; 8:4, 13–19; 11:10–12; 18:5–21; 20:4–29.
17. Dorsey, *Literary Structure*, 168.
18. Andrew E. Steinmann, "The Structure and Message of the Book of Job," *Vetus Testamentum* 46, no. 1 (1996): 88.
19. Vicchio, *Book of Job*, 57.
20. This interpretation of Elihu is not universal in church history, but then, no interpretation of Elihu is. The pseudepigraphal Testament of Job is perhaps the best known work to put Elihu completely in the camp of the Evil One.
21. Alter, *Wisdom Books*, 6.
22. Vicchio, *Book of Job*, 215.
23. G. K. Chesterton, *Introduction to the Book of Job* (London: Cecil Palmer & Hayward, 1916), xx.
24. Greg Boyd, "The Point of the Book of Job," ReKnew.org, October 16, 2018, https://reknew.org/2018/10/the-point-of-the-book-of-job/.
25. Hugh Ross, *Hidden Treasures in the Book of Job: How the Oldest Book in the Bible Answers Today's Scientific Questions* (Grand Rapids: Baker Books, 2011), 178–83.
26. Perhaps the greatest proof of this statement is John the Baptist, who *prepared the way for the Lord* not by doing any miracles but by calling people to repentance and pointing them to Christ.
27. Chesterton, *Introduction to the Book of Job*, xx.
28. That only the daughters are named in the end may be a prophetic foreshadowing of Revelation 2:17. The church is historically a female image.

Chapter 7 Kill the Wabbit!

1. Plato, *Apology, Crito, Phoedo, Symposium, Republic*, trans. B. Jowett, ed. L. R. Loomis (New York: Walter J. Black, 1942), 288.
2. "Actor Billy Crystal Pays $239,000 for Mickey Mantle Glove," CNN .com, September 28, 1999, http://www.cnn.com/US/9909/28/baseball.auction /index.html.
3. Melanie C. Green and Timothy C. Brock, "The Role of Transportation in the Persuasiveness of Public Narratives," *Journal of Personality and Social Psychology* 79, no. 5 (2000): 707.
4. See Hall, *Relational Spirituality*, 104.
5. Thomas Babington Macaulay, "Horatius at the Bridge" (London: Pearson Longman, 1842), 27.
6. Kenneth E. Bailey, *Jesus Through Middle Eastern Eyes: Cultural Studies in the Gospels* (Downers Grove, IL: IVP Academic, 2008), 279; italics in original.
7. Allen E. Lewis, *Between Cross and Resurrection: A Theology of Holy Saturday* (Grand Rapids: Eerdmans, 2001), 21.

Chapter 8 The Fourth Man

1. Iain McGilchrist, *The Master and His Emissary: The Divided Brain and the Making of the Western World* (New Haven: Yale University Press, 2019), 185.
2. L'Engle, *Walking on Water*, 17.
3. Robert Alter, *Strong as Death Is Love: The Song of Songs, Ruth, Esther, Jonah, Daniel: A Translation with Commentary* (New York: W. W. Norton, 2015), 214.

Chapter 9 The Sender and the Sign

1. Mark Twain, *Adventures of Huckleberry Finn* (Mineola, NY: Dover Publications, 2012), 77. Kindle edition.
2. Eugene Peterson, *Leap Over a Wall: Earthy Spirituality for Everyday Christians* (New York: HarperOne, 1998), 3.
3. Daniel Chandler, *Semiotics: The Basics* (New York: Routledge, 2017), 2.
4. Joseph Campbell with Bill Moyers, *The Power of Myth* (New York: Anchor Books, 2011), 5. Kindle edition.
5. Bailey, *Jesus Through Middle Eastern Eyes*, 280; italics in original.
6. Bailey, *Jesus Through Middle Eastern Eyes*, 283.
7. See Matthew 16:9, 11; Mark 4:10, 34.

Chapter 10 The Voice of the Storyteller

1. L'Engle, *Walking on Water*, 125.

Chapter 11 Resolving the Impossible

1. A variation of the three-plots idea is also attributed to Robert Heinlein and may have been referenced by Gunn in his lectures. See Sheila Finch, "Fantastic Journeys of the Mythic Kind," *Ad Astra*, no. 1 (2012), https://www.adastrasf.com/fantastic-journeys-mythic-kind-sheila-finch/.
2. Ernest Hemingway, *The Old Man and the Sea* (New York: Charles Scribner's Sons, 1952), 9.
3. Joseph Campbell, *The Hero with a Thousand Faces* (Princeton: Princeton University Press, 1949), 97.
4. Robert McKee, *Story: Substance, Structure, Style, and the Principles of Screenwriting* (New York: ReganBooks, 1997), 309.
5. Hall, *Relational Spirituality*, 242.
6. Gregory A. Boyd, "Christus Victor View," chapter 1 in *The Nature of the Atonement: Four Views* (Downers Grove, IL: InterVarsity, 2009), 25.
7. C. S. Lewis, *Surprised by Joy: The Shape of My Early Life* (New York: HarperCollins, 2017), 254.
8. Gustaf Aulén, *Christus Victor* (n.p.: CrossReach Publications, 2016), 17. Kindle edition.
9. Allen E. Lewis, *Between Cross and Resurrection*, 96.

10. J. R. R. Tolkien, "On Fairy-Stories," *Tolkien on Fairy-Stories: Expanded Edition, with Commentary and Notes*, ed. Verlyn Flieger and Douglas A. Anderson (London: HarperCollins, 2008).

11. Aulén, *Christus Victor*, 28.

12. Ben Pugh, *Atonement Theories: A Way through the Maze* (Eugene, OR: Cascade Books, 2014), 26.

13. Scot McKnight, *The King Jesus Gospel: The Original Good News Revisited* (Grand Rapids: Zondervan, 2011), 33.

14. McKnight, *King Jesus Gospel*, 69.

15. Leclercq, *Love of Learning*, 80.

16. Aulén, *Christus Victor*, 106.

17. Aulén, *Christus Victor*, 17.

18. Stephen Witmer, *A Big Gospel in Small Places: Why Ministry in Forgotten Communities Matters* (Downers Grove, IL: InterVarsity, 2019), 70.

Chapter 13 One True Story

1. Craig G. Bartholomew and Michael W. Goheen, *The Drama of Scripture: Finding Our Place in the Biblical Story*, 2nd ed. (Grand Rapids: Baker Academic, 2014), 22.

DANIEL SCHWABAUER, ThD, teaches English at MidAmerica Nazarene University and writes award-winning fantasy and science fiction novels. He earned an MA in creative writing under science fiction legend James Gunn and completed his doctoral work in semiotic theology with Leonard Sweet. He lives in Olathe, Kansas, with his wife and dogs.

Connect with Daniel:

DanSchwabauer.com

 @DanSchwabauer

 @daniel.schwabauer